THE HOUSE OF JOSHUA

Mindy Thompson Fullilove

THE HOUSE
OF JOSHUA

Meditations on
Family and Place

University of Nebraska Press
Lincoln & London

© 1999 by the University of
Nebraska Press. All rights
reserved. Manufactured in the
United States of America. ☺
Library of Congress Catalogu-
ing in Publication Data.
Fullilove, Mindy Thompson.
The House of Joshua :
meditations on family and
place / Mindy Thompson
Fullilove. p. cm. –
(Texts and contexts) Includes
bibliographical references.
ISBN 0-8032-2007-3 (cl.: alk. paper)
1. Environmental psychology.
2. Home – Psychological
aspects. 3. Public spaces –
Psychological aspects. 4.
Family – Psychological aspects.
5. Afro-Americans –
Psychology. I. Title. II. Series:
Text and contexts (Unnum-
bered) BF353.F85 1999
155.9'092–dc21
[b] 98–40577 CIP

This book is dedicated
to my teachers
Herbert Aptheker,
Estelle Schecter, and
Michael O. Smith
with gratitude for
who you are and for your
many kindnesses to me.

CONTENTS

ACKNOWLEDGMENTS

I am grateful to many people who helped me with this book. First and foremost there are family and friends—Maggie Thompson, Bob Fullilove, Bobby Fullilove, Kenny Kaufman, Dina Kaufman, Molly Kaufman, Fran (Crystal) Hale, Steve Crystal, Sally Crystal, Martha Stittleman, and David Himmelstein—who participated in discussions about the past and allowed me to share our stories. Without their support and encouragement, this book would not have come into existence.

Writing this book required a profound and painful confrontation with my past. My writing group helped me through that shadowy period by giving me healthy doses of emotional support along with their usual literary criticism. In particular, I am grateful to Adolf Christ, M.D., Grace Christ, D.S.W., and Lesley Green, M.P.H.

In addition to my writing group, professional colleagues read and commented on the manuscript. These included: Arthur Meyerson, M.D.; Estelle Schecter, M.S.W.; Laurie Lambert, M.F.C.C.; Francine Rainone, D.O., PH.D.; Julia Eilenberg, M.D.; Paula Panzer, M.D.; and Micol Rothman. Joyce Kobayashi, M.D., helped me decipher the connections among the situations described here. Lise Funderburg provided editorial advice. Cindy Brown, who has served as designer and illustrator for a number of my projects, helped me develop the concept for this book. A fellowship from the Open Society Institute provided me the opportunity to examine the interrelationship of race and space, thus pulling together the key themes of the book.

There are three authors whose works inspired me. I would like to thank Deborah Tall, who pointed out the need for a "psychology of place," Terry Tempset Williams, who demonstrated writing about family pain, and Kathleen Norris, whose work on monasteries answered some of my most puzzling questions.

I owe a particular debt of gratitude to Professor Sander Gilman, who has seen value in my work from the beginning. I have learned a great deal from him and I am honored that my book is a part of the series he edits, Texts and Contexts.

A number of people gave me permission to quote from unpublished writings: Bob Fullilove, Fran (Crystal) Hale, Kenny Kaufman, Molly Kaufman, Maggie Thompson, and Hannah Walcott.

Finally, a special round of thanks to my husband, Bob, who has lived with these ideas nearly as intimately as I have, and to my daughter, Molly, who proposed that I write about our family. To them I say, "If you have to write a book, do it with people you love."

AS TIME GOES BY: A CHRONOLOGY

Note to Reader: Place stories have little respect for time. This table provides the temporal order of births, deaths, and other life events.

1907	Aug. 12	Ernest Leroy (father) born to Joshua and Jennifer Thompson
1919	Dec. 20	Margaret Ailene (mother) born to Don and Minnie Brown
1942	June 6	Margaret Brown married Clifford Hunter (killed in action, 1944)
1944	Jan. 25	Robert Elliott III born to Robert and Helen Fullilove Jr.
1945		Margaret Brown Hunter met Ernest Thompson
1950	Oct. 15	Mindy Jennifer born to Margaret Hunter and Ernest Thompson
1953		The Hunter/Thompson family moved to Olcott Street, Orange, N.J.
1954	Jan. 8	Margaret Hunter married Ernest Thompson
1956	April 29	Meeting of NNLC leaders to dissolve organization
	May 30	Joshua Paul born to Ernest and Margaret Thompson Ernest Thompson lost his job with UE
1957	Sept.	Robert Fullilove III entered the Pingry School Orange school fight initiated
1958	Sept.	Mindy Thompson entered the Heywood School
1962	June	Robert Fullilove III graduated from the Pingry School
1963	Aug.	Crystal family home appropriated to build freeway

1964 Summer Robert Fullilove III worked with Mississippi Voter
Registration efforts
1966 June Robert Fullilove III graduated from Colgate University
1967 June 17 Robert Fullilove III married Evelyn Smith
(separated 1973; divorced 1983)
June Mindy Thompson graduated from Orange High School
1968 Jan. 10 Robert Smith born to Evelyn and Robert Fullilove III
Fullilove family home appropriated for proposed freeway
1970 July 29 Baby Boy Kenneth born and given up for adoption
1971 Jan. 25 Ernest Thompson died
May Mindy Thompson graduated from Bryn Mawr College
Aug. 21 Mindy Thompson married Michael Kaufman
(separated 1981; divorced 1983)
Dec. Mindy Thompson dropped out of doctoral program
at Yale
1973 Jan. 8 Baby Girl Dina Tracy Shepard born,
later released for adoption
1975 July 2 Kenneth adopted by Michael Kaufman and
Mindy Thompson
1977 Dec. 1 Dina Shepard adopted by Michael Kaufman and
Mindy Thompson
1978 May Mindy Thompson graduated from Columbia
University College of Physicians and Surgeons
1979 March 14 Molly Rose Thompson
born to Michael Kaufman and Mindy Thompson
1982 June Mindy Thompson met Robert Fullilove III
1983 July Mindy Thompson and Robert Fullilove III
moved to Berkeley
Dec. 23 Mindy Thompson and Robert Fullilove III married
1987 June Robert Smith Fullilove graduated
from Albany High School
1988 June Kenneth Thompson Kaufman graduated
from St. Mary's College High School
July Fullilove/Kaufman first vacation in France,
repeated annually thereafter
1990 Jan. Mindy and Robert Fullilove moved to Hoboken

1991 Aug.   The Fullilove/Kaufman family moved
             to the Thin House
1992 June   Dina Tracy Shepard Thompson Kaufman
             graduated from Hoboken High School
1997 June   Molly Rose Thompson Kaufman graduated
             from St. Ann's High School

ABBREVIATIONS

AIDS	Acquired Immune Deficiency Syndrome
BART	Bay Area Rapid Transit
COFO	Council of Federated Organizations
F&W	Farm and Wilderness Camps
FC	Flying Cloud Camp
FIPSE	Fund for the Improvement of Postsecondary Education
HUAC	House Un-American Activities Committee
NNLC/NLC	National Negro Labor Council
PH	Presbyterian Hospital in the City of New York
PI	New York State Psychiatric Institute
P&S	Columbia University College of Physicians and Surgeons
RFI	Radio France International
SAM	Saltash Mountain Camp
SNCC	Student Non-violent Coordinating Committee
UE	United Electrical, Radio and Machine Workers of America

THE HOUSE OF JOSHUA

INTRODUCTION

One Christmas, my husband, Bob, and I went to Newark, New Jersey, to spend the holidays with his mother. It was eerie to go from the hip and vibrant world of Berkeley, California, where we lived, to the postapocalyptic streets of downtown Newark. One day, we drove around in a rental car, looking at places we had known growing up. With snowflakes dusting the air, it seemed as if we should be able to dash into Bamberger's for a last-minute gift, but only the shell of Bamberger's remained. We drove past the vacant lot where Bob's childhood home had stood, demolished twenty years before to make room for a highway that was never built. Sad-looking men loitered in the park across from my mother-in-law's home, drinking from paper bags. We scuttled into the safety of her granite mansion, flanked by collapsing houses and armed with locks and alarms to keep the mayhem at bay. Our little red rental car, parked on the street, was stolen while we were inside.

That Christmas haunted me, a sense of dis-ease that was heightened when I moved back to New Jersey in 1990. As I wandered the hospital where I had studied medicine and the New York City neighborhood where I had lived for nearly ten years, I was pained to find that, like Newark, they were changed. It was unimaginable to me that my medical school could ask to see my identification card, but guards were posted at all the doors demanding proof I belonged. I couldn't get over the fact that the armory, which used to host high school track meets, had become a temporary shelter for a thousand or more homeless men. During the day, they milled around 168th Street, their despair spread like molten lead over the sidewalks. I shivered as I walked through Harlem streets hedged in on either side by crumbling apartment buildings. Sometimes a broken plaster face would peer back at me. "Help!" those once-beautiful faces seemed to say.

The contrast to Berkeley—where the houses were generally in one piece and the supermarkets sold edible vegetables—was shocking, and I wanted to know what people were going to do about the urban blight that seemed to be taking over. Much to my chagrin, the public health officials I encountered went blank when I mentioned the problems in the environment. "Hum, yes. Well, can't deal with that, can we? Too big," and they would politely switch the subject. It was implied, if not said, that I was breaking a social code by speaking of the unmentionable. The denial around me, the inexpressible consternation within me, and the sadness of the buildings pushed incessantly on my consciousness. In an attempt to name these queasy feelings, I began to look in textbooks and journals. Modern psychiatry has been preoccupied with the biology and physiology of the brain, especially as more and more drugs are discovered that can alter mood, thought, memory, and other cognitive functions. Not surprisingly, I found no ready answers in the journals I was searching.

It was while reading Deborah Tall's *From Where We Stand: Recovering a Sense of Place* that I had a profound awakening.[1] Examining Western cultural, literary, and psychiatric traditions, Tall argues that, for the past century, each of these traditions has tended to privilege time over place. As a consequence, we have developed a psychology that understands the temporal but not the spatial aspects of individual life. The thing that I was searching for, I realized, was a psychology of place. At the same time, I also understood that I would have to invent this new perspective on the mind in order to answer my questions. That is what I set out to do.

I turned, at that point, to John Bowlby, known principally for his work on the mother-child attachment, but who also had seminal insights into the relationships between people and their near environments.[2] Bowlby thought this near environment so important he called it an "outer ring of homeostatic mechanisms," as important to life support as the physiological homeostasis inside the human body. In Bowlby's terms, this near environment was an important object of attachment.

Alexander Leighton's work helped me delve deeper into this line of thinking.[3] Leighton's focus was on mental health in the context of community. His three-volume study of several small communities in Stirling County, Nova Scotia, revealed the powerful effects of the intimate environment on the life course and well-being of the individual. Leighton, like Bowlby, emphasized that the near environment was beloved, an object of what Leighton called "striving sentiments."

The striving sentiments, according to Leighton, are the basic human needs for food, clothing, shelter, love, belonging, and security. Different schools of thought, he noted, differed on the lists of needs and their relative importance. No matter: all agree that people do not exist in isolation but must fill their lives with contact with animate and inanimate objects. If they are not able to achieve these connections, if there is interference with the striving sentiments, distress will follow.

In addition to the seminal work of those two psychiatrists, I found work by geographers, anthropologists, psychologists, and urbanists that illuminated the issues of concern to me. In particular, I have pondered the ideas of sociologist Kai Erikson, anthropologist Anthony Wallace, geographers Edward Relph and Anssi Paasi, journalist Mary Bishop, and architect Christopher Alexander.[4] Perhaps the greatest consonance with the psychiatric literature was the respect each of these writers accorded the environment that surrounded the individual and created the setting for daily life. To this intimate world Relph gave the name "place," and that word, albeit irritatingly vague, has become a central focus of scholarly interest.[5]

What is a *place*? In the first sense of the word, place is a geographic spot that has a boundary defining its outer edge and an ordered plan to its interior. Synonyms would be *site* or *location*. When the word *place* is used by geographers, architects, or planners, it is this connotation they have in mind.

Paasi has challenged this dominant understanding of place.[6] In his view, place cannot be understood simply as a specific geographic location defined by convenient political boundaries. What is required is that place be understood from the perspective of the person's life story. Paasi's idea arose from his studies of the border between Finland and Russia. As a result of the unstable political situation between the two countries, the border has shifted from time to time, displacing area residents. Paasi found that the sense of self shifted along with these changes in political boundaries. Further, he learned the self of one political era had to be integrated into the self of the next political era, and so on.

As a psychiatrist studying place, I am drawn to Paasi's concept of place as the personal assimilation of "location" and "events." This evokes for me the police expression "We have a *situation* developing here." The analysis of situations, like the analysis of behaviors, thoughts, or emotions, is useful for psychiatry, since it gives important insights into human functioning. The questions that interest me include these: What are the core dynamics in the situation? How is the situation perceived by the protagonist? What are the long-term effects likely to be?

It is not easy, I have found, for people accustomed to thinking of situations as person-to-person interactions to acknowledge location as a factor in such stories. The following interchange (which took place by e-mail) is typical. Alex Cohen is an anthropologist at Harvard who shares my interest in place. He often forwards to me comments on place, such as this one:

It's out of context, but well placed nonetheless . . .

"The sight of London to my exiled eyes,
  Is as Elisium to a new come soule."
                    — Christopher Marlow
                    Edward II, Act I, Scene I

I responded:

Beautiful! What a wonderful place quote!

Alex wrote again:

My assistant, Laura, who is better read than I, says it is not about place, but rather about person. Here is the rest of the quotation:

"Not that I love the citie or the men,
But that it harbors him I hold so deare,
The king, upon whose bosome let me die,
And with the world be still at enmitie."

Who is right, Laura or Alex?

Laura is certainly right that this passage speaks of love. But Alex is also right because it speaks of love in a particular way, highlighting separation and distance. It is the speaker's cry to be reunited with the beloved that grips us in this passage. Consider this single word: *exile.* To be exiled is to be banished from one's native land. In many cultures, this is a punishment worse than death, because the awful pain of separation from home is an enduring form of torture. This is the subject Homer writes of movingly in the story of Odysseus, the most unhappy of men because he was exiled for ten years after the Trojan War.

Exile is about place in this regard: the self can never again be in the same place as the beloved objects back home. What produces the tension in the situation of exile is this particular location of self with regard to other places. Whatever is left behind is forever out of reach. The space that separates the self from the beloved is never diminished, never eliminated. The place the self now occupies lacks all that has been left behind. The sights, sounds, tastes, language of home are lost, except as cherished memories.

There are many such situation words: marooned, adrift, exploring, abandoned, isolated, pioneering. These are words heavy with emotion, words that carry a long history in their syllables. *Homesteading. Ambushed. Cabin fever. Long-distance love affair.* With a situation word, we are immediately oriented to the nature of the events.

That language is filled with situation words tells us something important about human existence and human psychology: these words are important in the language because situations are fundamental to human life. The self is always located somewhere, but the objects of the self's striving sentiments — to use Leighton's terminology — may or may not be nearby. Further, as I have already noted, the self is striving for not one but many objects. These objects include home, loved ones, work, and spiritual life, a quaternity I think of as "hearth, heart, grail, and soul." While it is possible to imagine a set of wants that pulls in a single direction, or wants that are all within reach, the more usual case is that the objects occupy different directions, obscured by obstacles or made inaccessible by forces beyond our control. It is the human condition, one might say, to "have a situation developing here."

To link situations to psychiatric theory, let me posit that what I call "a situation" is what Leighton would call "interference with striving sentiments." Because such interference can lead to distress, we can postulate that improperly resolved situations will lead to distress, as well. This leaves a number of unanswered questions. Given the many objects of our striving sentiments, is the nature of the distress dependent on the nature of the object? How does context ease or aggravate interference with striving? Is the distress proportional to the number of objects lost? Is joy determined by the number of objects gained?

In order to explore these questions and others, I undertook an analysis of my family's place stories. My family is important in this respect: my parents incorporated the ethic of hard work that characterized my grandparents into an ethic of hard fighting. Knowing that the color line was the problem of their century, my parents acted to erase it.[7] This action caused a rupture with the past, as Mom and Dad placed themselves against the mainstream of U.S. society. Along with thousands and millions of other Americans, they helped force a change in the course of events and the structure of our collective life.

The House of Joshua is the symbol of this break. The lineage of my family on my father's side continues, my grandfather's genes flowing through me to my children and grandchildren. But the actual house of my grandfather, Joshua Thompson, which stands on family land near the shores of the Chesapeake Bay, is a place my father left so that he might battle racism. He never took me there.

I think, in pondering the House of Joshua, of the story of the birth of Jesus. His parents, Joseph and Mary, had to travel to Bethlehem to pay their taxes because they were of the House of David. Yet in Bethlehem they had no place to stay, and they were consigned to a stable. The baby Jesus, born in those humble surroundings, made his first bed in a manger. In the case of that sweet infant, it was a House without a house. In my life, we have been a House with a house, but that house was not a home to all its children.

This book has nine stories, chosen because they were major situations in our family's collective life. As it turns out, each story is about a unique kind of striving problem: needing political power, family feuds, losing a home, spiritual searching. Together these situations reveal the sad, the sacred, the silly, and the salubrious events in a family's history.

The chapters are vaguely ordered by time. This is so because place events have a long trajectory, unfurling slowly as the years go by. The ancient Greeks felt that some relationships were so profound they would endure forever. Just as Castor and Pollux are eternally united in the stars, so some human constellations are visible long after the moment that formed them has passed away.

Each chapter reflects on a single story, reconstructed from memories and from family papers. My mother, Maggie Thompson, my husband, Bob Fullilove, and my children, Bobby Fullilove, Kenny Kaufman, Dina Kaufman, and Molly Kaufman, talked with me on many occasions about the book. I also talked to three members of the Crystal family, Fran, Steve, and Sally, and two medical school classmates, Martha Stittelman and David Himmelstein. The commentary offered by friends and family is expressed in the present tense ("he says"). The stories, because they are our history, are related using the past tense ("she said"), and recalled dialogue is framed in the past tense. The exception to this rule is that some of the stories were in process as I was writing the book. Telling and commenting merged as we tried to understand our lives in the midst of living them.

In meditating on these stories, I employed several strategies. One strategy was to identify a situation word or phrase that captured the essential elements of the story. This word became the title of the chapter.

Another strategy was to search through letters and other documents to find the earlier words, those that we had written about ourselves "back in the day" (or at least before I wrote this book).

From among those words I chose the chapter epigraphs. An expansion to other forms of representation was initiated by Sally Crystal, my childhood friend, who sent me an audiotape she labeled "Sounds of 10 S. Maple Avenue."

My third strategy was to locate archetypal versions of my family stories in myths and folk tales. Doing so enabled me to compare and contrast my family's experiences with those of other peoples in other places. For me, a real benefit of the archetypal stories was that they often contained a resolution of a complex situation. The brothers Castor and Pollux, for example, were inseparable in life and refused to be parted in death. Because one was mortal but the other immortal, this posed a problem for the gods. Jupiter resolved this by permitting them to divide their time between Hades and Mount Olympus. It is comforting, I find, to realize that many a modern couple has reached a similar compromise.

Examining family stories in this way turned out to be an experience richer than a mere academic exercise. This process of reexamination promoted a parallel process of reconnection among us and with our places. It is through this process that Bob and I have taken to revisiting Newark. If anything, Newark has become more desolate in the ten years since our little red car was stolen. As we stare out at the acres of empty land that used to be a thriving metropolis, we can label the flooding emotions: grief, disorientation, alienation, dislocation. As we name the emotions, we are also able to imagine a new future, a future in which houses and stores rise again, creating a new Newark that throbs with life and welcomes us home.

If there is any symbol that this dream might become reality, it is my mother-in-law's granite mansion, to which we fled that long-ago Christmas and which has become a community center that daily welcomes the citizens of Newark to congregate and to commune. Now known as the WISSOM Mansion, the house was adopted by a group of Muslim women who call themselves Women in Support of the Million-Man March. They have hung a set of photographs of Helen and Robert Fullilove, the ancestral owners of the house, in the hallway. I take profound delight in the loving care that is lavished on the building. There is an even deeper pleasure in the sense of gathering that goes on in the rooms of the house. Urban decay scatters people and tears neighborhoods apart. Standing amidst the little prairies, WISSOM Mansion is a bright spot of reunion.

Based on my research and this personal experience of reconnection, I would argue that the psychology of place is principally concerned with the sense of belonging to a locale. Our nation has struggled with two principal place metaphors: the endless movement to the new frontier and the limitations of the color line. Neither of these is a metaphor of belonging. Many environmentalists have associated the stripping of our nation's bountiful resources with our failure to establish a loving connection to our homeplace. I think they are right. The looming twenty-first century offers an opportunity for a new metaphor and a new relationship with the land. I hope that the story of the House of Joshua, which is so much a story of the dislocations of the twentieth century, will help illuminate a coming era of connection and belonging.

IN RETREAT

Homeboy and I went to a little place on John R. for our ribs. While we waited, we listened to some numbers on the jukebox, the last one a blues by Dinah Washington. Homeboy smiled, "Train, that was in memory of when I first ran across you. Train, there's one thing I want you to keep in mind, that's what I said to you tonight, for you will surely see it down the road. If you forget it, you will fail. If you can continue to hold on, and not lose sight of the ghetto, you will be a real part of the greatest battle of our times: the all out struggle for justice, dignity, and equality."

As we parted, dawn was breaking on John R. Street.

Ernest Thompson
"Homeboy Talks to Train in Detroit," 1970

The place story that I know best is my father's story. I know it so well because, at the age of nineteen, I undertook the task of helping him write his autobiography, *Homeboy Came to Orange: A Story of People's Power.*[1] That was shortly before his death, after he had been disabled by a series of strokes. My father was not a patient man, and I was not an experienced amanuensis. The small back bedroom of our house on Olcott Street was the setting for wildly melodramatic scenes we enacted with each other: my dad as annoyed with his infirmities as with me but yelling at me, me sobbing in my despair that I would ever figure out how to tell his story his way. Layered upon our theatrics were those scenes from other times and places that he wanted so much for me to see as he saw them, the scenes he wanted to record in his book.

The scene that was most difficult for me to describe was one from his youth. The facts of the story were simple. One summer, my dad planted some sweet potatoes that soon sent up green, leafy shoots. A

farmer's pig broke into the field and destroyed the young crop. My
dad and his father caught the pig and locked it up until the owner
could come get it. The farmer, a white man, came in his wagon, accompanied by a black farmhand. The farmer told his man to load
the pig into the wagon. He didn't offer to pay for the damage, as
would have been the custom in those times. My dad, incensed by
this maltreatment, ran into the house and emerged with his father's
shotgun. He pointed the gun at the white farmer and demanded payment. The farmer shouted to my grandfather, "Josh, take the gun!"
My grandfather Joshua talked to my dad and took the gun from him.
The farmer drove away without paying.

Those are the facts.

But how did it feel? I thought that my dad must have been outraged with his father for taking the gun from him. He said no, that
wasn't the way in those days. He didn't question his dad. But he did
enjoy the moment of power he experienced holding the gun on the
frightened farmer, and he swore he would have power again. But I
didn't get it: why wouldn't he be angry at his dad for not insisting on
getting paid? It didn't make sense to me. Living in a different world,
I had no idea what it would have meant for a poor, black farmer and
his teenage son to extract money from a white landowner. I kept
bugging him. He got annoyed because it was—to him—so obvious. Equally elusive for me was his vision of power. Not power from
guns, though he experienced the surge of strength because of a gun.
Rather power from asserting oneself, forcing one's opponent to back
down from one's might. My dad knew instinctively that many things
might yield that sort of power, and he wanted to find them.

Dad began his search in Hudson County, New Jersey, a heavily in-
dustrialized area just across the river from New York City. He was
tall for his generation, a lanky, loose-jointed fellow, with an awesome
intellect. He figured he could learn anything, and so he set out to
learn the ways of the big city. Early on he nearly lost his life, as he
liked to tell it, taking on a three-card monte operator. He studied
the man's moves for hours. When he was sure he knew the man's pat-
terns, he bet all the money he had. With a swift move, the monte
operator shifted the hidden ball. My dad saw the cheat, snatched

back his money, and ran away. The monte operator nearly caught him, but Dad was a fast, athletic country boy who outran his pursuers. Later, Dad met a professional gambler who took pity on him. The gambler told him, "Boy, you got to learn to survive in the big city. You ain't never gonna be slick, and you too country to learn to cheat. So if you gonna play with cheaters you got to be able to take care of yourself. I can't teach you how to cheat, but I can teach you how to keep the cheat off you."

Dad took his lesson to heart, and it became a core part of his image of himself: the country boy wise to the cheat. He liked to play up his homeboy image, because it lulled the suspicions of the cheaters. Whether he was negotiating with three-card monte operators, or the executives of General Electric, his down-at-the-heels country look belied his capacity to see the cheat and defeat it. He paid no attention to his clothes, other than to make sure that his cap was on his head before he went outside. Always more or less disheveled, with odd pieces of paper and York Peppermint Patties falling out of his pockets, he looked like every other homeboy in the ghetto. Half dozing in a meeting, he did not look to his opponents like someone who should be taken seriously. Their error, obviously. He was a powerful and canny politician, capable of leading and winning massive campaigns for black power and human rights, usually against the odds.

He started organizing from his own interest in bettering the situations in which he found himself. He had more heart than skill at the beginning, and his first few efforts were defeated. But he gained expertise quickly and soon emerged as a leader in the explosion in unionization that swept the country in the 1930s. In 1943 he became the first black paid organizer for his union, the United Electrical, Radio and Machine Workers of America (UE). Convinced that the strength of the union depended on eliminating discriminatory practices, Dad was part of an aggressive campaign for fair employment practices for minorities and women. In 1950, he became the national director of the UE's Fair Employment Practices program.

At the same, in conjunction with black labor leaders in the UE and other unions, Dad worked to build a new organization, the National Negro Labor Council (NNLC, or NLC for short). The NNLC led important campaigns to desegregate Sears and Roebuck, the airlines, and General Electric's Gateway plant in Louisville, Kentucky.[2] Dad often commented that the Gateway campaign, designed to prevent a runaway plant from taking advantage of racism and low wages in the South, was one of the most exciting and successful campaigns he had experienced.

Aside from the good work he was doing, Dad was living a pretty remarkable life. He had a travel card from the union that allowed him to go all around the country on his Fair Employment Practices work; he was hobnobbing with the most brilliant men and women in the trade union movement; and he was winning fight after fight all around the country. He was called Big Train (or simply Train) by his peers because he could deliver the goods. If money was needed to start a campaign, he had the union behind him. If people were needed, he knew where to get them. More than that, he was a formidable strategist with two decades of experience in labor and political struggles to contribute to any discussion.

But it was not to last. The UE was brutally attacked as part of the McCarthy-era Communist witch-hunt in the 1940s and 1950s. In 1956, the union split into two parts and Dad lost his job.

The NNLC was dissolved to prevent a costly and fruitless legal battle with the Subversive Activities Control Board. When the NNLC leaders met on April 29, 1956, for the last time on John R. Street, many wept. They vowed to be true to the principles of the NNLC, with one important difference. Instead of looking to the labor movement for their base of support, they would base themselves on the ghetto. "Retreat to the ghetto and come back strong!" was the motto they adopted that night.

"Retreat to the ghetto and come back strong" represented a radical reorientation. Dad often scribbled stories about his mythical hero, Homeboy, who educated him about the ghetto. "Homeboy," Dad wrote, "told me, 'Man, never forget that your hope and your source of strength lie with your people here in the Black ghetto.'" In a story Dad wrote, "Homeboy Talks to Train in Detroit," Homeboy "schooled" Dad to build his base in the ghetto, not in the union movement.

The story opens in Detroit.[3] Dad had arrived there to plan for the opening convention of the Negro Labor Council. He was too excited to stay in his hotel room, so he set out down John R. Street. Suddenly, in front of the famous nightclub, the Flame, he heard the familiar voice of Homeboy. After spending some time in the glamorous setting of the nightclub—Joe Louis was at the bar and Willie Bryant was playing—they stepped out into the night.

Standing amidst the crowds on John R. Street, Homeboy said, "Train, you seem convinced it's time to pool the experience and militance of Negro workers in the cause of equality. I think you're right. I hate to tell you this, man, if you don't base your efforts on the ghetto, you'll lose."

"Why you say that, Homeboy?"

"Train, is it true that you base your hopes of winning this struggle of black labor on the union leaders and the full support of the left?"

"Yes, what's wrong with that? This is the new ingredient the cause needs, because as you can see, nothing's happening."

"That 'new ingredient,' as you call it, sure would be great, if you were gonna get it. Just think of it, black labor hitting hard, backed by organized labor with all-out support from the left—ol' Homeboy would be happier than you for better days for the ghetto would not be far off. But your ingredient will not be put together."

Dad argued with Homeboy, but Homeboy kept pressing him on every front. Homeboy's most telling point was that Dad and other black union leaders had glamorized their new opportunities in the unions. Bill Hood, Homeboy pointed out, might have a great job at the United Auto Workers Local 600 in Dearborn, but "not one black man, woman, or child lived in Dearborn."

"Dig yourself, Train, how often did you say to yourself, 'How great can I get?' Train, after twenty years in the foundry, you ought to know better."

Dad wrote: "I could only say, 'Homeboy, you scored.'"

In the story, Homeboy's promise that Dad would make his greatest contributions to Negro freedom from a ghetto base was framed by the dawn breaking on John R. Street.

But Dad didn't feel much hope when he actually found himself trapped in the ghetto of Orange, New Jersey, with no influence and no power. His fall from power was sudden, and he sat for some months licking his wounds in shock and dismay. My mother saved him from despair when she pointed out that the schools were segregated by districting lines that played havoc with the geography of streets, cutting out and enclosing enclaves so that whites would be with whites and blacks with blacks. I was then a second grader at Oakwood Avenue School, an all-black school formed by a crazy districting system. Dad had never forgotten either the pig that had destroyed his garden or the big white farmer's blatant abuse of power. Enraged by a new encounter with that same old disrespect, Dad reentered the fight.

THE GHETTO

There is a sameness to black ghettoes, however large or small. There are bars and churches—sin and salvation—shoulder to shoulder on nearly every block. There are a few stores, an occasional soul food restaurant, a funeral home, maybe a doctor. There are lots of kids, playing, yelling, dancing—black people are a people of the drum, and rhythm is foreground in the lives of children raised on patterned chants, clapping games, and dance steps. There are buildings clinging to life by a wish. If there is a little land, someone has pushed some tomato plants and some seed corn into the soil, just as my dad did behind our house. Down the side streets and back alleys the needle-users and the transvestites reign. The wall dividing ghetto from not-ghetto is as distinct as if it were made of brick and mortar.

For my dad, the tangibleness of the wall around the ghetto was the defining experience of his life. To see on a map the manner in which the white-powers-that-be had decreed the limits of his freedom was intolerable. Dad came to Orange because he was defeated on the national scene. Its provincial narrowness deepened his despair—he felt keenly the loss of the broader arena, even just the bigger ghettoes of Hudson County and New York City—but its sameness drew him back into the struggle that was his life's work: defeating the cheaters.

Three places might be said to define the contrasts in Dad's life: the Eastern Shore of Maryland, where he discovered injustice; Hudson County, where he learned how to get power and achieved some of his greatest successes; and Orange, where he acquired wisdom. The process and the learning were inseparable from the places in which they occurred. It is this sense of place that is so important in understanding my dad's life. The shape, the form, the essence of the ghetto were woven through his life and his work. The ghetto was the stuff of his metaphors and his dreams. It is impossible to understand the logic of his life without naming him a man of the ghetto. In fact, "Homeboy in the Ghetto" was the working title of his book, *Homeboy Came to Orange*, for many years.

Ghettoes are among the most emotionally charged places on earth. They are the physical manifestation of the power to enact hatred, to confine the despised other to a walled-off place. The ghetto enfolds its inhabitants, whether they are Jews, gays, blacks, or Chinese. But if the walls are created on the outside by hatred, they are decorated on the inside by love. As long as any capacity for resistance exists, those walled into the ghetto make it their home. In the Lidice ghetto in the former Czechoslovakia, in New York's Chinatown, in San Francisco's Castro District, people have made of their small portion a nourishing home. Think, if you doubt this, of Anne Frank pinning pictures of movie stars to the walls of her room in her family's hiding place.

Yet, as we are reminded by Anne's story, the resistance struggle is not always successful. The ghetto, created by the hate and power of those on the outside, can be destroyed by them at will. When the Nazis destroyed the ghetto at Lidice, they razed the town and plowed under every remnant of its existence. It vanished from the earth just as ruthlessly as it was created. For all the homeboys in all the ghettoes, place is made of the endless tension between the oppressed's will to live and the oppressor's wish to murder.

The ghetto is a place in which we live and dream. But it is not simply the scenery for the events of our lives. It is a major actor in our lives, shaping our day-to-day experiences and molding our internal reality. Through this lens of the ghetto, I have learned about the power of place to shape the ways we think and feel.

You can, for example, trace the politics of identity in black communities in the United States by watching the evolution of the character Homeboy. Long before I learned to read, I was taught the importance of "Homeboy" by being forbidden to draw on Dad's work and by being allowed to help my mother arrange and put away the pages of Dad's manuscript. Dad's Homeboy was a variation of the character of Simple, the everyman proposed by Langston Hughes, a laughable buffoon, raunchy, raucous, and endearing in his bumbling efforts to adjust to city life. Much as Dad laughed at Simple, he could not identify with that character. His own hero was a visionary who used simple country stories to teach people enduring truths. His Homeboy was the embodiment of wisdom, not buffoonery. Dad wrote of his hero, "Homeboy is more than a natural man. He's a symbol of the bond between men and women in the black ghettoes everywhere." Homeboy was to my dad what Athena was to Odysseus: an occasional visitor empowered to keep him safe, lead him home. Homeboy was kind, patient, and farseeing, a mixture of qualities that contained none of my dad's shortcomings but all of his strengths. When I began to help him with the book, it was clear that I couldn't write the tales of Homeboy. Slowly, the book ceased to be the story of his mythical friend and became the tale of Homeboy Ernie Thompson.

With the closing of the great migrations from the rural South to the cities of the North, South, and West, I thought that the concept of Homeboy would be lost. Instead, as it has gained currency among the youth of the ghettoes, it has taken on a new incarnation. "Homeboys" are still defined by that critical characteristic of coming from the same place — "He knows where I'm coming from." But this generation's Homeboy is neither the simple man Langston Hughes invented decades ago nor the mythical freedom fighter my dad envisioned. This generation's Homeboy is a survivor. He has been thrown out onto the hard streets of the inner city, and he has mastered its brutal realities. He is deeply connected to others like him — his homeboys — but he is just as profoundly disconnected from the outside society.

Stephanie, my brother Joshua's wife, told a story of sitting next to some homeboys in a fancy restaurant. One young man became enraged when the waiter gave him a cloth napkin. "Man, this ain't no napkin. I want a napkin. Bring me a napkin." In this allegiance to a world in which napkins are made of paper, he asserts loyalty at all costs to his roots; he allows no room for assimilation. Dad's Homeboy was sophisticated and cosmopolitan. Today's Homeboy is rude, crass, and limited. Today's Homeboy has turned his back on a world that does not want him: he looks inward at the ghetto and takes it for his own. When Dad and his homeboys were defeated by McCarthyism in the 1950s, they vowed to retreat to the ghetto and come back strong. To the extent that their comeback faltered, these modern homeboys are the inheritors of a world created not by Martin Luther King and the civil rights movement of the 1960s but rather by anticommunism and its assault on the union movement in the 1950s, a terrible blow to equal employment opportunity from which ghetto communities have never recovered.

Once I heard the voice of Homeboy, my dad's old friend. I heard him say, "Brag is good dog, but Hold Fast is a better." I wrote down his words. Shortly after I finished, my mother knocked on my door to say that Dad had died. That country saying was not one of my dad's favorites; it was rather a minor theme. But through the years of holding fast that lay ahead I was often comforted by Homeboy's advice. If the homeboys of Dad's time valued Hold Fast, these modern homeboys favor Brag, their flashy gold chains and big cars a new way to claim and hold the territory of the ghetto. It is, for our communities, a new chapter in the struggle to endure.

Each of us needs a place on the Earth, and, when we can, we want to improve our place. Some are greedy and steal the land of others. Some are weak or weaponless and cannot fight for what we have. The strivings for place take on a dimension that is far larger than the wishes or will of the individual. Groups—tribes, clans, castes, cities, nations—battle for land and the resources that it holds. In these conflicts, groups win or lose, and the individuals are carried heedlessly along. Place may be defined as a setting, as a set of social interactions, or as a node of the life biography. Whatever the definition, place is always a matter of politics. Each place has porous boundaries that interact constantly with other places that fill the world. In order to understand the politics of place, we must always understand one place in relationship to other places. The identity connected to a place is comprised of the "here" that is attached to the place, but also the "there" that adheres to the rest of the world. These identities are in a constant state of tension and interaction. Further, they make and remake each other as people within each place ponder and adjust their relationships, or even alter the places themselves.

It is worth emphasizing that this politics of place is not simply the layering of social and political groups onto a passive landscape. Geographic structure is itself a force that pushes events along. This force of geography lies in its capacity to demonstrate the order of the world as well as its chaos. For example, we can map the neat array of post offices, or gas stations, or distribution networks, and they will demonstrate logical relationships to population centers or other characteristics. At the same time, those lines of order lie one next to another, creating a whole that need not be logical at all. The rationale for placing a post office may locate it next to a pornography shop, not because letters and X-rated movies have anything in common, but because each, in relation to some other structure, fell there on a local map. The simultaneous creation of order and chaos is the power of geography, the very shape of the world of politics.

The politics that govern place have two salient characteristics. First, all places are assigned to people and all people are assigned to places. The true meaning of being "out of place" is that one has stepped out of an assigned spot. The homeboys in the restaurant were "out of place" by their own as well as by society's definition of turf. Their misposition was marked by their demand for a paper napkin in a cloth napkin establishment. In making place assignments, those in power take as much space — as well as the best-quality space — as they can get. Those who are productive workers, creating needed goods and services, are given second-best places. Those who are not productive — the disabled, the frail elderly, and the criminals, all groups that have greatly expanded in our postindustrial society — are given places only marginally suited to support life.

Second, places are assigned by power relations, and the "quality" of a place is derived from the "quality" of people assigned to be there. The places of the poor are regarded as "bad" places, the places

of the rich as "good" places, without regard for the actual constitu-
ent elements of the place itself. Thus, urban renewal can dismantle
tracts of housing, simply by establishing that they are places where
poor people live. The odd planning strategy of displacing the poor—
without regard for where they will go—makes sense only in a model
of the politics of place that assumes the poor are not entitled to a
place, that they are, by appellation, placeless, and hence do not re-
quire dedicated territory. The growth of homelessness in the United
States and the parallel growth in displaced peoples around the world
support the sense that the politics of place has been transformed
into a politics of no place. This is, essentially, a strategy of genocide,
however cleverly it may be disguised.

People need a place in order to live. To deny a place is to deny life.

That place is political does *not* mean that the individual is political in any conscious sense of the word. It only means that decisions
about place are made by groups in conflict with each other. Tribes
and institutions and societies control space, not individuals. Even the
powerful individuals who seem to own the land do so only with the
support of their social group, and only as long as their group retains
power. The individual is always at the mercy of the political decisions, some made nearby, others made far away, that create the social
geography that structures the potential life pathways of each person.

That place is political *does* mean that the individual—constrained
to a narrow spectrum of the world's places—has internalized a sense
of place that carries with it all the baggage of winners and losers. The
winners get to feel good, and the losers are made to feel lousy. Julia
Eilenberg, a psychiatrist in upstate New York, makes the point that
you know you're in a country town when you're not on the Weather
Channel anymore. Rural America, no longer the center of national
life, has settled into a state of invisibility that is lifted only by tragedy
or disaster. Because people identify with the places in which they live,
the loss of standing has led to a profound collapse of self-pride. It is
not just the weather map: it is all the undercurrents of conversation,
the jokes, and the silences, that create boundaries, letting people in or
keeping them out. A small town in South Carolina, site of a famous
murder, was made uncomfortable by all the attention it received.

People worried that it was creating an unfavorable image of a close-knit village. They banded together to fund the trial of the accused woman. "We're going to do this right," said one townsperson. "We don't want them thinking we're a bunch of turnips fell off a truck."

While visiting in Roanoke, Virginia, in May 1995, I met Arleen Ollie, whose family lost its home when urban renewal destroyed black communities in Roanoke.[4] She shared with me her sense that the adults in her community were left with a pervasive sense of shame. The loss of community could not be discussed because it was too painful. It was too painful not only because these people had lost tangible things—homes, businesses, churches—but also because they had lost their land, their children's inheritance, and they could no longer be proud. Ollie was convinced that the weight of shame that lay on the community was a central feature in its current dysfunction.

Shame and rage can be seen as two sides of one coin, in which the degradation of one's place becomes an essential element in the hopes, dreams, and feelings of the individual, in fact, in the very image of the self that exists in the mind of the individual. Garrett O'Connor, an Irish expatriate psychiatrist who works in Los Angeles, links this malignant shame to drinking and domestic violence among his countrypeople. The same is probably true of other displaced peoples around the world.

It is an important proviso that those most thoroughly injured are people who accept the judgment placed upon them by others. Those who question, who seek to define themselves, may succeed in creating something different. The insider's attachment to the land can act in opposition to the devaluation of "poor" people and their land imposed by outsiders. The internal love fights with the external label in an ongoing psychic battle. It is the attachment to the land that makes the battle so fierce: if it didn't matter, no one would get upset. But it does matter. In fact, it matters greatly. Returning to the homeboys in the restaurant, their alienation from the mainstream culture is deep. They experience the cloth napkins not just as "different" but as "insult." In demanding "my" kind of napkin, they defend their land and their people.

COME BACK STRONG

Dad's struggle to keep his promise and come back strong after the demise of the NNLC and losing his job with the union began with his 1957 effort to undo school segregation. From that beginning, he worked with friends to build political power in the ghetto. He used that power to build coalitions to address displacement due to a freeway, jobs campaigns, and the establishment and protection of representative government. In his last years, his efforts went increasingly into claiming land. One of his most dramatic struggles was to build a new high school. Our town had a mediocre school system run by people who didn't care. As far back as 1935, accrediting bodies had criticized the high school for overcrowding and failure to serve the needs of the majority of students. Yet for all those years the local board of education had ignored warnings that those deficiencies might lead to a loss of accreditation. Further, the problem was a carefully guarded secret that came to light only after Dr. John Alexander, a pediatrician representing the black community, was appointed to the board. The city residents, then, had their first chance to find out what was going on. In 1964, the County Department of Education had said

> We have very serious reservations about the adequacy of the high school plant. In our opinion it is not possible to operate an effective broad program such as is needed in Orange today in the present building. The following conditions are cited:
>
> ... there are too few classrooms to permit the reduction in the size of large classes because the school is already being used beyond its functional capacity;
> ... there are no remedial classes;
> ... the library is about half the size it should be;
> ... the art room is totally inadequate;
> ... the same may be said of the clothing room;
> ... the metal shop and the wood shop are both incapable of handling more than a small minority of the students who could benefit from such experience.[5]

Alexander immediately asked for an evaluation from the state Department of Education, which found the building absolutely inadequate to house the number of students and the activities to which they were entitled under state law. What was needed? Dad was impressed by the fact that 20 percent of students—those with me in the college track—were headed for higher education. But the majority— 80 percent—would be seeking work immediately after graduation, and there was no trade for which they were prepared. The "training" offered in woodworking and sewing in that school was wildly outdated. Further, it was clear that the world of work in the future would be changing rapidly as technology advanced. My dad was the first person I knew who talked about the need for constant learning, retraining for new jobs every few years, and basic education as the foundation for a lifelong process of adaptation. I have lived to see every bit of his prophesy come true. At the time, however, few could believe that the world they saw around them wouldn't last. There were still factory jobs in the area, and in those days an unskilled worker could always depend on a job pumping gas. It required a massive campaign to convince the city leaders and the voters that building a new high school was essential for our town.

Envisioning the new high school was a long and exciting process. It involved developing a shared sense of mission, a sense of the purpose of education. The board of education adopted a philosophy of "comprehensive" education and developed a mission statement that opened with the words "We believe in the worth and dignity of every individual." How do you enact dignity in the concrete of a school building? For Orange, the crucial change was that the 80 percent of the students entering directly into the work force were to have facilities as rich and supportive as those available to college track students. Vocational shops were to be up-to-date, they were to feel real, they were to be connected to the world of work as it existed in the immediate community. This ultimately meant big work areas, new kinds of labs and shops, lively classrooms, all supported by state-of-the-art libraries and media centers.

Dreaming of a new kind of education, one that prepared all children for the future workplace, was one thing. Funding the school was another. As the plans for the school evolved, the problem of getting a bond issue passed by the school board budget committee and then by the city council loomed large. By then Dad was very ill and was hospitalized during periods of the campaign. Yet it was his finest hour, the moment his Homeboy had promised him so many years before. Every skill Dad had ever developed, every instinct honed, every bit of wisdom he had bought with age, went into that fight. Dad had a remarkable ability to read situations and to develop campaigns that reworked the existing elements into a more democratic vision of the future. The campaign slogan, "Let's not economize with our children's future," became the core message that was to be carried to the voters of Orange.

What the campaign depended on, and the story that is the focus of *Homeboy Came to Orange*, was the development of an effective coalition. The school fight would affect the ghetto, but it could never be won by the ghetto alone. Dad's core team, representing the black community, was impressive. It included Board of Education President John Alexander and City Councilman Ben Jones. But allies of every sort were needed. Years of making political alliances had built all sorts of connections throughout the town, and those relationships now came to the fore. From a core set of political relationships, many dating back to the original school fight at Oakwood Avenue School in 1957, the struggle for the high school became a mass movement of townspeople concerned about providing the best education for their children. It came down to confrontation between the elite, who didn't care, and the majority of people, who did.

This confrontation took place in the era of the long, hot summers, when race riots swept through American cities. It was the year Martin Luther King Jr. was killed, precipitating mayhem in cities across the nation. The threat of riot also hung in the air of Orange. On a hot August night in 1968, the city council met for the crucial vote. Fifteen hundred people were in the auditorium at Central School where the meeting was held. On one side of the stage were white racists, led by Anthony Imperiale.[6] On the other side of the stage were the United Brothers, a group of young black militants. Throughout the hall were police with billy clubs, riot helmets, and mace cans. Television lights blazed, increasing the heat. In the high school stadium, a mile away, half-tracks stood on alert in case the vote went the wrong way and the pent-up emotions exploded in a conflagration.

Speaker after speaker went to the microphone to urge that the city council pass the bond issue.

Alexander, as president of the board of education, spoke first. "We have fooled around long enough. Give our children the high school they need!"

Michael O'Neil, a white executive who as a leader of the Labor-Business-Industry Committee supported the school, said, "Stop playing with education and let's get that new high school!"

Reverend Russell White warned the council, "You're playing Russian roulette, and the bullet is in the chamber tonight."

Harvey Glover, a high school student, pleaded, "Why don't you just do right?"[7]

There was a brief pause at the high point of the drama, as the city council recessed for ten minutes. Ben Jones, the only black person among the city councilmen, exhorted his fellow council members. "We have to vote now. We have no more choice. We're under compulsion from the state, we've had in-depth studies, and this is what we have to do. We have to build that school. We have to come to that agreement, except that some of us say it's too expensive. I submit that if we fail to pass the resolution tonight, it will be more expensive than any of us ever dreamed."

In the following minutes, the council, recognizing the power of the people arrayed for the new high school, voted yes. The auditorium broke into bedlam. The people had won! Ben Jones, when I interviewed him for my father's book, told me that later that evening, after the hugs and the cheers subsided, he suddenly realized that quiet had descended and he was alone. He walked with some trepidation into the night, but the peace of Orange filled the streets. It was safe. Dad and his team had won.

In December 1970, we organized a reunion of veterans of the National Negro Labor Council. My dad's words to his old partners-in-arms were captured on an audio recording of the meeting:

> I went a couple of years ago to help the Packing House Workers in a runoff election in Maryland. My sister, brother-in-law, and so on were in the union and about a hundred cousins. When I got to my sister's house—my grandfather's house—my sister sat and cried, said, "My *own* brother gone make me lose my job."
>
> Down there in the countryside the Packinghouse Workers and the trade union movement did not see [that] in the county there was a black majority and in the county seat an overwhelming majority. And yet the black people had no power and fear reigned the countryside. Fear has not left the countryside. I hope that our projection in Orange—we started with 20 percent of the population—will be a guide to people on the countryside. . . .
>
> NLC did not have political power. When we retreated to the ghetto, you couldn't leave the ghetto if you had no political power. I hit the ghetto cold in Orange with zero and came back strong. So I come to testify and say we have written a book to this testimony, dedicated to the Negro Labor Council's ideas.

Coalition politics to build safe places was the ultimate message of my dad's life and of his book. Ernie Thompson, a refugee from rural poverty and family violence, had thought a great deal about place, and in particular about creating places where black people could prosper. Over the years he became convinced this could happen only by learning to make common cause with people of other groups, that is, through coalition politics. Coalitions are built on shared concerns. They are important because they meld the power of otherwise distinct groups. Minorities, he knew, cannot win in isolation, but they can break their isolation through coalition. Though my dad was from the ghetto, the logic of his life was to overcome its restrictions. He believed that he had the right to marry a white woman because she was the one he loved. He was convinced he could be friends with people of all races, religions, and creeds. The ghetto was the source of his power, but the point was not to stay in the ghetto. The point was to have an effect on the broader politics where the fate of the ghetto was really decided.

It was somewhat unexpected that the politics of coalition led to a politics of friendship. Over the years he found that there were many people who wanted more than superficial political connections: they were searching for friendships with people different from themselves. These days, the United States is neither a melting pot nor a tossed salad but rather the crossroads of the world. Everybody from everywhere is here. There are classrooms in New York City in which each of thirty pupils speaks a different language. Though the variety can be bewildering, it also has a breathtaking charm. Simple formulas about white and black are irrelevant when one is faced with a hundred different cultures, or a thousand different cultures, or maybe more. The diversity is hard to imagine, but one touches it constantly. It tears at the old assumptions of difference. It makes us wonder.

And we must embrace with enthusiasm that wonder. It needs direction and encouragement, but it is a new and unimagined hope for a different, more tolerant future. This is not to say I think bigotry has been defeated. But I think that bigotry, and the fear it represents, is inherently less interesting than the kaleidoscope of cultures arriving in our ports. Coalition politics have, at a minimum, the capacity to support the search for common cause. Beyond that, there is always the potential for genuine human respect to cross artificial boundaries of race, color, or creed.

The psychology of place teaches us that the individual cannot be separated from the politics of the world at large. Coalition offers the dispossessed the best hope of staking a claim for a place on the Earth.

My father left me his message of coalition as a parting gift. "Go everywhere and tell them about coalition," he said to me. At his memorial service his close friend John Alexander gave the main eulogy. He told me before the service, "I'm gonna rock the house." And he did.

LOVE-TORN

Mon., July 5, 1965

Dear Mindy—

I have a wool shirt for you and will mail it tomorrow.

I arrived home Sunday morning and have been having a nice visit with my father, mother, sister, uncle, and some cousins. . . . My uncle is talking about sending me to law school days so I could get through sooner. He has $135,000 and says he wants to do some good with it. But it will never happen. . . .

Love,
Maggie

Monday, July 12, 1965

Dear Mindy,

I arrived back home yesterday morning, to find Ernie really quite sick. Dr. Kingslow has been seeing him. Also gather there was some kind of incident at Camp Calumet and the two Hopson girls came home. I don't have the details yet. Altogether a lovely homecoming!

Why have you not written? Really this is inexcusable. . . .

Did you like the shirt?

Love,
Maggie

Friday, July 16, 1965

Dear Mindy and Josh—

Here's a good joke for you: once upon a time a cowboy was dying. He was a stranger in town. The other cowboys gathered around him and said, "Tell us your name so that we can let your mother know." As he drew his last breath he said, "My mother knows my name."

Love,
Maggie

The house of Joshua, from my perspective, was founded by my mother who did something pretty unusual for the 1950s by becoming the white unmarried mother of a biracial kid—me. This bold move horrified her parents, who refused to acknowledge me as part of their family. My mother's life was thereafter divided into two parts, only one of which I could enter. This meant my mother had a secret life and I had no grandmother.

Of my two parents, it was easier to know that I couldn't figure my dad out. He was reticent about his feelings and told about himself only through certain moral tales, which, actually, we heard endlessly. He told them well, so we were never bored of hearing them. But they were not designed to reveal the inner man. When asked a question he had a tendency to be cryptic, giving one- or two-word answers to the most intricate questions. I once read that all black men felt emasculated. I asked him if he thought he had been emasculated. He stared at me coldly and asked in reply, "What do you think I think?" That was the end of that conversation.

It was harder for me to realize that I didn't really know my mother. She was my ally, my buddy, my conversation partner. But there was a whole part of her life that existed away from me. In 1950, when I was born, my mother began her life as Persephone.[1] Like the Greek goddess who divided the year between her husband's home in Hades and her mother's home on earth, my mom went back and forth between two worlds. For fifty-one weeks of the year she lived with us on Olcott Street, which, at least to me, was a lot like living in hell, but it was really just a little ghetto community. For one week of the year, she traveled home to her mother and father in the all-white world of Ohio. Minnie Hall Brown, the Demeter of this story, filled her daughter with love and good food, took delight in her presence, then sent her back, nurtured and replenished.

The deal struck with the devil was that no one in Ohio was to know that Maggie Brown Hunter, the war widow, now had two biracial children, a black husband, and a new last name. "They never told me to say that I was unmarried," she says, "but there would have been a lot of explaining to do."[2] Instead, she did her explaining to me. Her parents were nice people and I would love them, she said. She never said I couldn't meet them. That truth emerged from the years of watching her depart alone, leaving a McConnellsville telephone number in case I needed her. She was grieved when I rejected a doll sent by this grandmother who wouldn't meet me. There was a kind of logic to her that she had chosen a life different from what her family could accept. She was proud of her choices, and she was willing to pay the price for them.

I was not. I spent years composing the perfect letter to Minnie Hall Brown, the letter that would make her want to know me. Later, the letter was only meant to punish. I wanted to damn her to hell for refusing to be my grandmother.

We needed a grandmother badly, and we didn't have any. My father's mother, Jenny Comegys Thompson, had died when he was a young teenager, leaving for him a lifelong ache and for me a void on the grandmother front.

One reason we needed a grandmother was Senator McCarthy and the Cold War. My parents were "progressive," our catch-all phrase for the Communists, Socialists, labor organizers, antinuclear agitators, civil rights leaders, and others who wanted justice and equality. A decent wage for a decent day's work. Equal opportunity for all Americans, regardless of race, creed, or color. In the 1930s and 1940s the many progressive movements had organized unions, integrated baseball and the armed forces, struggled to defeat fascism, and promoted women's liberation.

In the 1950s the opposition struck back. They made *Communist* a four-letter word. To have that word attached to your name in any way, shape, or form could cost you your job, your home, your community. The highest levels of government joined in the witch-hunt to stamp out labor unions, peace marches, civil rights, and women's equality. So much for freedom of assembly, freedom of speech, and freedom of the press. Once the progressive movements had been deemed obscene, they ceased to be part of legitimate—even valued—public political debate. Instead, they became the object of an antipornography campaign.

Our little family was under the enemy spotlight for many years. The FBI sat in cars outside our home. They frightened the neighbors with tales that we were "Reds." They stood in the lobby of my mother's office building. As she headed home, exhausted from work, they would approach her. "Mrs. Thompson, can we speak to you?" "No," she would say firmly and walk on, outraged but frightened.

Under the onslaught of hearings and firings and convictions, the progressive community slowly disintegrated. Grief and terror filled peoples' lives. It became impossible to speak openly about ideas. The FBI was everywhere. And the Red scare stirred up other Americans to join the witch-hunt. After a performance by Paul Robeson, the great African-American actor and singer, in Peekskill, New York, the buses and cars of concertgoers were stoned as they left. Many were injured. All were frightened. Was this what it would cost to have independent ideas in America?

Not everyone was willing or able to pay the price, and so the retreat began. People fled in all directions, hiding their radical pasts however they could. As the flood tide of reaction receded, it left people stranded in places like Orange, New Jersey.

There were lots of rules about being radical in Orange, New Jersey. There were things we said and thought at home, and then there was what we could say outside. In sixth grade, during one of the local election campaigns, I was reading a book of modern Soviet short stories. This was definitely a "home" book, but I took the book to school one day. During some boring school activity, I took it out. I carefully arranged my desk so I could read without the teacher seeing. I often did this to speed the passage of time, since listening to my classmates stumble over words or numbers was intensely irritating for me. I knew the dangers of reading clandestinely well enough to remain alert to what was happening in the classroom so that I could respond as needed.

That day, however, I became entranced by a story about a woman who had lost her first husband during World War II and later remarried. One day, her first husband showed up, and she had to choose between the two men. The final lines of this enthralling story describe her resting her earth-stained hands—she'd been working in the garden—on the shoulders of her current husband. That was the ending.

This was too cryptic for me in the sixth grade. I was sure I had missed something. I started reading it again. I was going through the story for the fourth time when one of my neighbors leaned over and said, "The teacher's calling on you." I gasped in horror—now I was in trouble.

She asked, "What are you reading that's so interesting?"

"Nothing."

"Why don't you let me see it?"

I was in deep trouble. MODERN SOVIET SHORT STORIES. In the middle of the Cold War. In the middle of a local election campaign.

I had to surrender the book to her. She looked hard at me. "Do you think this is what you should be reading?"

That answer I knew. "No," I mumbled.

"I'll keep the book for now," she said.

I stumbled back to my seat in agony. My parents were going to kill me, and I still didn't know which man the character had picked with her earth-stained hands. (Of course, it's quite obvious—she picked the new one, but I didn't figure that out until I reread the story twenty years later.)

Again needing something to read, I returned to school that afternoon with *The Road to Life*, by A. S. Makarenko—a great story about abandoned boys who were given a new life in a very disciplined, but loving, school shortly after the birth of the Soviet Union—but I was much more careful. My dad, on hearing about this, sternly grilled me, "Do you know what you could have done to the election campaign if this got out?"

It is hard now to imagine that kind of fuss over a book. But such books were banned then, and the penalties for transgression were stiff. The injection of a Red scare into the election could have undermined years of work by Dad and others. I knew the rules, and my carelessness was not acceptable. Ours was a life of secrecy.

And yet it was not. All the time my parents were promoting some cause or another, constantly pushing the envelope of what could be said and how it might be expressed. There were certain core values of American democracy that remained inviolate during those years. Senator McCarthy and his witch-hunters could never convince the American people that racial segregation was compatible with "liberty and equality for all." Coleman Young, a colleague of my dad's in the NNLC and later mayor of Detroit, played that ambivalence when he was called before the House Un-American Activities Committee in its hearings in Detroit. He had the following interchange with Congressman Jackson of HUAC:

> Mr. Jackson: You said that there is a whole lot wrong with all the world.
>
> Mr. Young: I am interested in the United States and not the whole world.
>
> Mr. Jackson: Let us not lose freedom—
>
> Mr. Young: That is the point, Mr. Jackson. I am fighting for freedom myself.
>
> Mr. Jackson: So am I. Let us not lose individual freedom and human dignity by sacrificing it to an order of things which has filled concentration camps to overflowing. If you think of the lot of the Negro who have in eighty-some-odd years come forward to a much better position—
>
> Mr. Young: Mr. Jackson, we are not going to wait 80 more years, I will tell you that.
>
> Mr. Jackson: Neither are the Communists. They say they are going to overthrow the government by force and violence and effect all the changes immediately.
>
> Mr. Young: If you are telling me to wait 80 years, I will tell you I am not prepared to wait and neither are the Negroes.
>
> Mr. Jackson: Neither is the Communist Party.
>
> Mr. Young: I am speaking for the Negro people and for myself. Are you speaking for the Communist Party?[3]

Civil rights, in fact, gained steam during the McCarthy era. *Brown v. Board of Education* and early sit-ins were both expressions of the continuing fight for equality for African-American people. But being against capitalism, for socialism, against imperialism, for national liberation were all taboo for the time being.

Another reason we needed a grandmother was the pressure of circumstance that weighed more and more heavily as the years went by.

Once, as I was developing some extravagant plan to move someplace, my dad said, "I don't think people have that much control over where they live." We had been stranded in Orange by such workings of the gods. My mother moved into a black community because that was the only place where we could live together. She bought a house in Orange because it was the only community we could afford. In 1953, when the three of us settled on Olcott Street, Dad was a nationally recognized leader of the labor movement. His dislike for Orange didn't matter much because he traveled so often. In 1956, when he lost his job with UE, we had no choice but to make a home in Orange.

My mother, having chosen the house for its lovely views of the park and its tree-filled backyard, was perhaps happiest to be there, but she had an odd position in the community. Everywhere, my mother insisted on being "Maggie." Neighborhood children, brought up to use titles with adults, would address her as "Mrs. Thompson." "Just call me 'Maggie,' " she would tell them. I used to wish she didn't need to be different. It made me feel that she was a white lady trying not to lord it over us.

My mother was very neighborly. We lent and borrowed, shared garden produce, and helped with chores. She did not, however, have many friends. Those who weren't afraid to be friends were unique, independent people like Murl Peters Daniels, who balanced heart-of-gold with in-your-face as tidily as I have ever seen. This was life on the margins, being white in a black world. My mother's best friend during my growing up years was Fran Crystal, who was a WASP like my mom, and intermarried like my mom, though Fran's marriage to a Jew was nowhere near as outside the rules as what my mother had done. Neither Fran nor her husband Dan had been exiled from their families, and they moved in a large circle of people. We lived in a small circle, saved from isolation mainly by my dad's political associates and a few old progressive friends who, like my parents, refused to give up the struggle. The kindness and companionship of colleagues and comrades kept us from complete isolation.

Despite the grim surroundings, Mom set up housekeeping with resolve. My mother was a fan of light housekeeping. She thought most cleaning was a waste of time. Her motto was, "When company is coming, clean the bathroom last. After all, no one can see what's going on!" The book *I Hate to Cook* was in tune with this point of view and struck Mom as so funny that she would laugh until tears ran down her cheeks. On the other hand, she loved to *create settings*. She moved furniture frequently. She spent eleven months of the year planning the color scheme of the house and one month bringing her vision into reality. She planted flowers, watered the grass, arranged lamps, and hung paintings. At times, her passion rose to the heights of art. We lived across the street from a park, so we had lots of light and the constant play of the seasons. My mother had a big picture window put in that made us feel as if the park were the extension of our front lawn.

Within the warm nest she created played my little brother, Joshua Paul, and I. Our weekly building festival always climaxed in the demolition of our skyscrapers made of several hundred wooden blocks. Josh and I used to turn wicker chairs into tents, zoo cages, houses, and rest zones, typically laying them on their sides and covering them with blankets or sheets or other building materials. We hauled out our books and toys and records and left them conveniently in the middle of the floor. My mother clung to the futile idea that by putting our things on the stairs she could get us to take them up to our rooms. Her struggle against entropy was never-ending.

Just as my mother tried to create order at home, she tried to create it at work. Shortly after my birth, Mom began to work as a legal secretary for Morton Stavis, who had a general law practice at 744 Broad Street in Newark. For the next forty years, and in more ways than I can list, he was a rock in her life and she in his. However bohemian her life appeared, she carried the old-fashioned Yankee work ethic. For his part, Mort's appetite for work was ferocious; Mom matched his strength by the force of her will, but she often came home nauseated with fatigue. Still, she was back on the job the next morning, finding and correcting every undotted "i" and uncrossed "t."

She could not tolerate imperfection on the job. When really exasperated with someone's carelessness, she would complain, "What kind of lousy way is that to work?" For my gentle mother, this was a colossal rebuff. At work—I've already noted her ideas on household chores—she was a big fan of the poem, "Do your work as well, both the unseen and the seen. Make the place where gods may dwell, beautiful entire and clean."

My mother was, in the early years, able to manage the enormous load of home, neighborhood, and work. She delighted in us. It's not unusual for mothers to love their children and to be proud of them. Some mothers, perhaps many, even build the world around their children. My mother was both in love with us and dependent on us. There was such a little world outside of the three of us: my dad, Josh, and me.

If such a constellation could hold, it might have worked. But, instead, it succumbed to the force of entropy. Without a grandmother to give advice, free meals, and infusions of cash, our little family could only turn inward, and there was only so much we four could do.

I had real proof, I thought, that the grandmother idea would work: Gram, a real grandmother to other people, lived in a big house at the corner. Stone lions guarded her front door, and she used to babysit for us. She had a big, quiet house that was always spotlessly clean and dark. We played Buck Rogers with the old cabinet radio on her porch. We lived for the days on which she would bake rolls. She initiated the tradition, which I carry on, of making a strawberry shortcake for Josh for his birthday.

Gram was good to us, but she was even nicer to her own grandchildren: they got rolls all the time! I was sure our own Gram would have made a difference in our lives.

Instead, everything depended on my mom's ability to keep everything going and to keep everyone happy. There were moments when it seemed as if we might make it. Some happy letters survive in which we were all trying to make the best of it, as in this missive I sent.

> July 9, 1963
> 10 S. Maple Avenue
> EO, NY

Dear Mom,

How are you? How is Grandma? I hope she is all right. Say hello to Aunt Lou Ann for me, Thanks. . . .

My typing and my flute playing are improving tremendously. As I get there early every day (Dan drives me), Mr. Quinland gives me practically a private lesson until the others come. I can keep up with Band IV now almost easily. . . .

Josh's trunk is at the station and Fran is going to pick it up and pay for it, and drop it off at camp for him.

I have decided that I am going to ride over to the Crystal's house every morning and thus save myself $.25.

It was good to hear your voice! I'll be very happy when you get back. Don't however rush yourself because all is fine here and we are all well. Besides you need the vacation. . . .

                                                              Mindy

But my mother was carrying a lot, and the load became heavier with each passing year. She was the sole financial support of our family after Dad lost his job in 1956. She had to take care of the house. She pushed herself relentlessly on the job. She did much for others, with little time for herself. In fall 1964, when I was in ninth grade, she started to go to law school at night. I was thrilled by this new venture. I wanted my mother to want something for herself, and it was exciting to see her try. She would come home bubbling about torts and contracts. She studied hard. She did well.

The household routine, however, was thrown into chaos. The cooking and housekeeping were thoroughly at sixes and sevens. My dad could cook a few dishes but was not an enthusiastic homemaker. While Mom was at law school, he was, often as not, at a meeting. I was deep in the throes of my search for (1) identity and (2) a boyfriend, not necessarily in that order. Josh missed the time and attention that had always been lavished on him. He just cried whenever Mom was around. Dad got sick that summer with the first of many illnesses that were to plague his last years.

Things at our house unwound. After a year, she decided not to return to school. "I probably could have managed all those things," she reflects, "but I actually didn't want the responsibility. I started to think about the lives that would be in my hands and I didn't want it." She thinks of this as a "Cinderella complex" after a book that was popular. I don't know if it was a complex, but many progressive women were struggling with those issues. They had vivid ideals. They had been swept into the joys and agonies of the political life. Yet they carried the nurturing and the tenderness for the movement. It would be an exaggeration to say that there were no men who were kind and patient with children. But many of them carried the weight of the political discourse. They had to decide what was "politically correct"—and what was politically correct meant a lot to people influenced by the organizational ideas of V. I. Lenin. Women, in the world I lived in, nodded at the political line and did what felt right.

That, for example, was certainly what my mother did when she became pregnant with me. It was an accidental pregnancy. She and my father could not marry because he was still entangled in a bitter divorce. It certainly wasn't politically correct. But she didn't give a hoot what any politico said: she was having her baby.

Like many progressive women, my mother's "feeling politics" were invisible. It is not recorded in any history book that early in 1950 Maggie Hunter, née Brown, decided not to have an abortion. It simply didn't—still doesn't—count as a political act that she would defy so many people to live as she chose. It was in just that way that my mother's politics were overshadowed by my dad's activities. On a typical week, the local paper in Orange would have five stories related to Dad's activities. My mom, in the interim, had washed dishes, read bedtime stories, played music, and shaped our young consciousnesses to reflect her own radical ideals.

These lived politics were deeply influential. My mother was often distraught, but she was never mean. She was honest to a fault. She would have given the shirt off her back. I remember one Christmas when she gave away a new set of dishes. They were lovely brown dishes, but she knew that her friend Fran admired them. She sat for hours. She would put the dishes in the box. Then take them out. Put them in the box, take them out. Finally, she put them in, wrapped them up, tied the ribbon, and said to me, "Fran has done so much for me, I know this will give her joy."

This quiet life had a different aesthetic from the aggressive world of the law. But it had too few pleasures. Studying law had been a pleasant dream, if not the right one, and there were not other dreams to take its place. That I was preparing to go to college undoubtedly intensified my mother's grief of that period. My birth had got her into Orange, but my leaving certainly didn't get her out. It was the start of a long depression for her. The pressure on me increased enormously: I was to live out the dreams she couldn't manage. The whole law school effort might not have mattered so much if there had been more give in the system. As it was, the isolation from her family, the loneliness of her daily life, and the pressures of too little money were unrelenting.

The summer of 1966, when Dad turned fifty-nine, we gave him a big birthday party. At the end of the party, my mother sat in the kitchen, sobbing desperately. From there our family began a long, agonizing unraveling. We four seemed locked together in a horrible nightmare. For years the four of us tumbled in free fall. Our family had no life outside of our house. We hardly ever went anywhere together. When we did, it was awkward and uncomfortable. We did not have a rhythm for liking each other while moving through space. In fact, I don't think we liked each other much at all. My parents drank heavily during that time, which made them coarse and abusive. My brother retreated into a succession of fantasy lives that left him progressively more and more disengaged. I cried, pouted, begged, and threatened suicide. Whatever good the early years had held was submerged in the hot agony of our failure.

My father's illness, which had become serious and unrelenting by 1968, reconfigured this scenario, our rage giving way to guilt and sorrow. He became kinder and gentler as his disabilities progressed. By the end of his life, he was a good guy. His death, coming as it did at the moment of his redemption, did not free us, but rather left us longing for him. It was years—ten for me—before we three survivors regained some semblance of normalcy.

About a month after my dad died, my mother's father died. She left to go to the funeral. It was one more time she left us to go to them. She must have loved her father enormously, but that was not something I could imagine. The emotions connected to the times and places of her white family were emotions beyond my comprehension. I couldn't imagine missing the man—I couldn't imagine the man.

That is, at the heart of my relationship with my mother, always the biggest conundrum. Who are you? I often want to ask. Like a hazy crystal ball, her emergence into adult life is forever out of sight. I can't imagine life on a dairy farm, with horses to ride and a wonderful lake to swim in. I can't picture the two-room schoolhouse where she rose to the top of her class. Equally impenetrable is the college she attended, the professors she liked—the past is incomplete. My Persephone is like a spy who came in from the cold. For me, she has only a present and a future.

My mother's father, whose death I did not mourn, wanted to be a lawyer. He went to law school at night, enduring great hardships. At that time, his wife, my grandmother, was sick with a severe kidney ailment. He nursed her, did the chores, took care of his two daughters, worked long hours at his job, and went off to class. Whatever that effort cost him, I do not know. I do know that, by the time he finished, the state had changed the laws so that lawyers were required to have a bachelor's degree. He had not gone to college, and now it was too late.

Is it a coincidence that my mother, like her father, reached for but did not attain a career in law? It's an intriguing question. What I do know is that it lies in the shadows of her life, a place to which I have no access.

Despite the pressure and the isolation, my mother's happiness did not collapse entirely or disappear completely. She always maintained a certain clarity about her choices. As far as I can tell, this was rooted in a childhood experience of shame. A young black boy who was her classmate and the only black child in town came to her home to visit. Her dad called to her, "Margaret, your little nigger friend is here." She was mortified and hid, refusing to acknowledge that she had a "little nigger friend." Seventy years later this memory makes her wince in shame. She tells me this story in a hushed voice, afraid of my judgment, though I have heard it many times before and have never been as moved by it as she seems to think I would be.

Her sense of the "race problem" was enforced by a series of experiences she had as a student at Muskingum College. When she began to agitate for admission for black students, she was called to the administration office and warned that, if she didn't stop, she would be expelled. On another occasion, a black man came to speak at the college. He was unable to use a restroom or eat on the seventy-mile trip from his home to the college. Horrified to learn this, my mother took him to her sorority house for dinner. Her sorority sisters were aghast, but she was much more concerned with feeding a tired, nice man than with their views of propriety. After college she visited the South to see what this "race problem" was all about. The more she learned, the more deeply she became convinced that there had to be an alternative. She intuitively found her way to antiracism as a way of life.

Her choices were fortified by her real interest in other people. She has what I call "a thirst for diversity." She liked people from other countries and other places and wanted to get to know them. When she saw a person treated unfairly, she became angry. She abhorred injustice and was happy to learn that she could fight it. She was determined to meet prejudice head on and not to fail as she had as a child. She threw herself at those barricades daily for all the years of her exile. She was clear, nearly always I think, that this was what she wanted.

How do you throw yourself at barriers? My mother had several styles. One was frontal assault, typically her style with other white people. A salesclerk would fail to see that she and I were together. My mother would say, "This is my *daughter.*" She would smile proudly and squeeze my hand. Another was to retreat into jocularity. This was more typical of what went on when black people were around. She used humor as an icebreaker, a joke's-on-me sort of maneuver. She was often the butt of jokes, letting her ignorance of black language and culture serve as a foil, setting off outraged cries of "*Maggie!*" She laughed along with us as we laughed at her. Over the years it became —or perhaps it always was—more a form of hiding than joining.

Whatever the limitations of her actions, they represented her choice to be a loving, progressive person. It is perhaps the combination that is unusual. Out of her love sprang the impulse to keep the warring parts of her family with her. Out of her progressive ideals came the need to separate herself from the limitations of her family of origin and to bond with a man she found courageous and correct in his beliefs.

From her perspective, this is all very straightforward. After all, she inhabited the irreconcilable parts of her world. My mother, as Maggie Brown, went every year to spend time in the places of her childhood and with the members of her family. She had the opportunity to work and rework the memories of now and then, to stir the pots of past experience, to connect with her other world. My mother, as Maggie Thompson, lived in Orange, New Jersey, with us. She created our little world and kept it together as best she could.

Yet, for me, the partition of my mother's life had other meanings. My mother has the appearance of being the most open person in the world. In fact, she is just that. But the structure of the world holds parts of her in places I cannot go. It creates a mystery: I do not know the troubles she has seen. I believe that, like Persephone, Mom did her best to manage the problem of loving irreconcilable people. And perhaps because she disappeared into pleasing all of us, she remains unknown.

WAYLAID

Once upon a time there lived a turkey named Tom. One day Tom the turkey went for a walk. He walked and walked til he could walk no longer. Then he saw some food but it was only a nut. Then O how he wished he was safe on the farm with the other turkeys. Then he saw something moving along the road and then he saw a little girl her name was Betty and she was picking flowers for her mother. She was very poor.

Today was Thanksgiving. When the girl saw the turkey she ran after it and the turkey ran away from her too! But at last she had him and that was the end of Tom the Turkey.

Mindy Thompson
"Tom the Turkey," 1959

By gradual steps, children come to know place beginning with the discovery of their own toes and extending through time and space into the wide, wide world. In infancy the world is linked tightly to Mother. In early childhood it lies within sight of the house. In middle childhood it extends into the near fields and woods and playgrounds, often centered on a self-made home, like a fort or a den. In adolescence it opens wide, as far as one can go and return in a day, preparing the young person for the day when she will leave and make a new home in a new place.

The spiral of movement from the first home to the world develops outward in an orderly fashion. At each step of the way, the growing child learns new skills for managing the world: new skills in navigation, in being with friends, in meeting strangers, in learning new customs and languages. As with all developmental tasks, the timely completion of each stage is a prerequisite to good progress in the next. My spiral to the world was knocked off kilter because I lost my school when I was seven.

The first part of my childhood was nearly all nice. The first place I remember is my crib, which was located under a window in the back bedroom of our first-floor apartment. I remember a moment of great pride as I drank from a cup. Then I lay down and tried to drink again. The water felt cold as it spilled over my face and pajamas, and I was filled with acute embarrassment. It was at that moment I understood the difference between a cup and a bottle. In those days, I liked to wear my mother's high heels (and nothing else, my mother points out) and walk up and down the sidewalk in front of our house.

My world enlarged to include school, and I have many memories of the Community Chest Nursery School that I attended for a couple of years. I had a friend, Raymond. We thought of ourselves as Roy Rodgers and Dale Evans, and we coveted guns and boots and bullets. We were deeply envious of a classmate who had a bandanna full of bullets. One day, Raymond and I were the last ones at school. We found our friend's bullets and decided to keep them. Raymond took the silver ones. He said, as he was Roy Rodgers, that he deserved them. As Dale Evans, I had to be content with the red wooden ones. I count that day as the birth of feminism in my life.

Another fine day, we fulfilled a lifetime dream. We loved making crumbs of graham crackers and longed to have a whole package to break up into pieces. One day we found a neglected package at school and learned that indeed it made a remarkably tall pile. We were quite proud. Imagine our surprise when the teacher came along, grumbling and annoyed, and threw our crumbs in the garbage.

My mother came to school one day with her Rolleiflex and took photographs of us painting, washing our dolls, climbing, and sitting around. I was very proud of her pictures and glad to have her document our world. The photographs lifted us out of the ordinary. We were, after that visit, preserved in black and white for future generations to learn how to go to nursery school.

Each year there were more places in the repertoire of my memory. I was shy but happy. I liked the world. I liked frogs and swimming. I liked barbecues in the backyard. I liked thunderstorms in the summer and snow in the winter. I liked school.

I liked *my* school, Oakwood Avenue School in Orange, New Jersey. I remember hopping to school, remember school as something to hop to. Hopping because you had to jump over the cracks in order not to break your mother's back. Hopping because some paving stones had crosses in them and those stones you had to jump over entirely: the crosses seemed to carry some very special message, as if we could read runic letters and communicate with the ancients who had carved the news for us in silky gray slate. Hopping because at school we played hopscotch with passion and intensity, searching for the right stone to throw, one that would fly through the air, landing surely, not glancing off the number, but resting soundly and reliably, and then hopping to retrieve that stone and keep it in your pocket for a day or a week or until it was lost and you had to find another one. Hopping because going up stairs to class was a passage in which we converted giggling brown selves into quiet studiousness, a passage strewn with betraying laughs under the sharp eyes of the teachers and the hallway monitors who could disgrace you if the giggles hopped out. Hopping like the facts that were jumping into my mind as if they couldn't wait to be learned and then hopping out quite unpredictably, like trying to remember Frosty the Snowman had a very shiny nose and and and. . . . The facts always seemed to hop out just when you thought you could most depend on them to be there.

I didn't know or care about the silly map that made my mother so furious. I know that she went to the board of education to get the map. My mother is a mild-looking woman who inspires trust, so of course they gave it to her. I imagine that she brought it home to my father. "Ernie," she said, "you have to do something."

My mother means it when she says that. You can argue with her if you want to, but you might just as well give up. Aside from Dad's anger at Jim Crow, I bet he was just nagged to death. I have experienced my mother's fervor when she gets what he used to call "a bee in her bonnet." So Dad took on the Orange School Board and crushed them. Out of the joy over that victory arose a campaign for John Alexander, my pediatrician, to be mayor. For the first time in Orange history, a black candidate chosen by the people was running for that office.

My life had been filled with hopping before, but I was even more joyous when the campaign headquarters opened. Suddenly, as if it had always been there, the headquarters appeared at the corner just as you came out of the shadow into the sunlight. The campaign headquarters was very shiny. The paper was shiny, the buttons were shiny, the people laughed and guffawed in a delicious, embracing way. And no one said "no" when you went back every day and got another shiny button. No one said "you took one yesterday," they just laughed and guffawed. Every part of the campaign was shinier and more exciting than the part before. The ice cream, the barbecue, the motorcade. I sat in an immense convertible, feeling very satisfied that, as we drove through town honking and calling, everyone would look proudly at me in the car and I would look proudly at them from the broadness of the cool leather where I sat.

That was a wonderful, joyous period. We were doing something grand, I knew, from the smiles on the faces of the adults around me. I did grand things, too, from time to time. I wrote a leaflet. I left flyers at my neighbors' houses. I was happy to be a part of what I knew to be a moment in history.

But I had no wish to do more than that.

I was shocked to learn that my parents wanted me—expected me—to be part of the school desegregation they had fought to win. They wanted me to give up my world, my warm segregated school, to go to a new school on the *hill*, where the *white* people lived. It was not in our neighborhood. It was high and big, not our kind of place. It was far. Someone who clocked the distance on his car odometer said the schools were equidistant from our homes, but never in all the years I walked back and forth was I ever convinced of that. It was *much* further to Heywood Avenue School than it was to my Oakwood Avenue School. I did not want to go.

The itching came in the summer. In the summer there was no hopping. Life seemed too big and too hot. Too itchy. At day camp it seemed hard to keep up with people. When the itching came I would feel overwhelmed, as though I would have to claw my skin off to find peace. Finally I learned that by supreme will I could ignore it and it would run its course and pass yet be the only existing experience of the world as it swept my body. One day, after the itching passed, I fainted, feeling the blood rush from my head, leaving it empty and floating as my stomach rushed up to fill the hollowness.

But the headaches were yet again worse. I knew that they followed the rage, a screaming, impotent rage that I would hurl at the world. And the rage was followed by tears of such force that I felt I would lose myself in them. The headaches would not come the day of the rage, however, but the next day, I wondered whether I couldn't bring on the headache sooner by taking a nap. That way I could get it over with and be well the next day. I don't remember why I needed to be well, but I do remember that my plan didn't work. The headache was there in the morning as it always was the day after the rage. It tore at my eyeballs and drained weak and feeble tears. It engulfed my stomach. Motion was intolerable. Light was intolerable. Time was intolerable.

The day before I started my new school I cried. For once, the headache didn't come the day after rage, but the second day after the rage. I was sick for several days. I did not feel like hopping to school anymore. School was strange. The only other black person in my class was Stevie from around the corner. But Stevie had little to say; he rather searched the world from behind the protective plate of thick glasses. I felt very lonely.

My teacher had a device for teaching us good habits. It was a big "apartment" house made out of cardboard, very like the graphic at the beginning of the Late Movie, with a window cut in it for each student. At the beginning of the year she had us each bring in a picture and put it in a window. Then we had to carry out a number of good behaviors, including brushing teeth, eating citrus, and going to bed by eight o'clock. Every morning you had to report. If you had not done all those things, your window was closed for the day.

I became fanatical about this. I once ate a lemon because it was the only citrus in the house. One time my mother took me with her to collect money for the Mothers' March of Dimes. It became clear that we were not going to get home on time. I made my mother flag down a police car so I could get to bed by eight. On at least one occasion I was forced (as I saw it) to lie. But the gravity of lying mattered little compared to the fear of having my window closed: then I felt terrible shame and loss. It was all too much.

The new school was a strange place for me, and I couldn't get a foothold. I had had a plan for fitting in at Oakwood, but at Heywood I never knew what to do. The pain of dislocation was so intense that I gradually retreated more and more into a world of my own creation. Robert Coles, in his writings on children who desegregated schools in the South, has tried to understand how they were able to withstand the awful indignities to which they were subjected by white mobs.[1] I experience those stories with nearly the same wonder he felt. How *did* they do it? I was deflated by loss and overwhelmed by the challenge to adapt. I focused on surviving. I constantly told myself that there would be a happy ending some day. In the interim, I became the hero of my own story, a figure-skating star or great actress, in a tale that started in the morning before I even opened my eyes and ended only after I went to sleep.

The story of my alternate life as an ice-skating star was largely a device for moving through space. Waking up, brushing my hair, walking to school (especially), being in gym class with no one to talk to: those were the times that I slipped into my own universe, away from the awful awkwardness and ineptness that my isolation engendered. When I could sit, I read. My mother had collected a rich and varied library that introduced me to the classics. When I was old enough, I went to the Orange Public Library, whose cool, quiet presence was a balm. I fell even more in love with the Newark Public Library, which introduced me to the augustness of learning. There, the long reading tables and high ceilings created in me the sense that I had room to think and need not fantasize. Books and dreams, then, became my world.

Lincoln Steffens, in his autobiography, makes the point that getting a horse shaped his childhood. Instead of joining in games with other boys, he started a more independent life of adventure and exploration.[2] For me, the abrupt shift in my world turned me inward and away from social interaction. Going places was largely intolerable, meeting people burdensome. Thinking was my most accessible pleasure.

Around age twelve, this alternate universe seemed to dissipate, as if a fog had lifted. Probably this occurred because I was given a small bit of life that I wanted to live: the world of The Theater. Roz Wilder, who directed the Pied Piper Teen Theater Workshop, took me into her world of improvisation and production even though I was a little too young for her classes. She might have guessed how desperate I was. The theater was an amazing discovery. Until then, alternate worlds had only been in my head. Now I could actually be *in* them, at least for moments at a time. I had no great gift for acting. I could barely be myself, much less someone else. I was awed by performers, though, especially when it came to expressing loud, transporting emotions. The five years I had lived in my head had left me with a social disability: I was clueless about real life. The theater provided a bridge back. Through our work in improvisation, Roz taught us what people did. Most of her students were learning to act. I was learning to be.

Much as it helped, it nevertheless failed. I couldn't find a place in the theater. I was a tall, plain, tan girl with short hair, hence I spent my early adolescence as the understudy for the male lead. Around the age of fifteen, I went to see *Oliver!* on Broadway. At the end the cast sings a rousing conclusion, "Consider yourself one of us! Consider yourself part of the family!" I wept to myself that the only part of the theater family I would ever be in was the seats, watching, and that was not enough.

I knew that I was a child of crisis, a tender warrior. I had done the right thing; I was the pride of my race. My early showing as a race hero gave me inflated hopes for what I would achieve in life. I didn't want to be in a place like the theater, where race would so define my opportunities. I didn't want to watch: I wanted to be grand. One day my high school biology teacher, Mr. Amen, said to one of my classmates, "You should study biology because you're really good at it." He didn't say it to me. I wanted to be welcomed like that.

But it was never so simple as someone saying "Come with me." While in college at Bryn Mawr, I had a wonderful Spanish professor, Mrs. Paucker, who was so impressed with my quick mastery of the language that she invited me to spend the summer with her in Spain. I couldn't understand the invitation, and so I didn't go. The real toll of the five lonely years was an enduring suspicion that no one else's place could be mine.

Ambition and suspicion remained with me as the dual lessons of school desegregation. Obstinacy and terror. Fearlessness and phobia. It is a puzzle to understand why I abstracted two seemingly contradictory emotions. In third grade, I was chosen to read the Bible at the school assembly at which my class was putting on the Easter show. My parents gave me a beautiful new Bible from which to read. It was an illustrated Bible, and I was particularly gripped by the beautiful painting of Esther approaching the throne of her husband, King Ahasuerus.

The story of Esther is my favorite Bible story. I often celebrated the Jewish holiday, Purim, with my friend, Sally. Purim celebrations re-create the story of Esther. I used to love to dance the part of Esther in those celebrations. I felt her power as if it were my force. I paid little attention to her fear.

But the Old Testament does not neglect that part of her story. As all familiar with the Book of Esther will remember, Esther was called on to save her people, who were to be massacred at the instigation of the evil Haman. Esther's uncle, Mordecai, told her, "You must go to your husband, the king, and plead for the Jews."

"But you know that I can't go to him unless he sends for me," she replied. "To go without permission is to risk death."

"If you don't go, you will die, as all the Jews will die," he countered.

Realizing she had no choice, she told her uncle, "Then tell my people to fast and pray for me for three days. My maidens and I will pray and fast, as well. On the third day, I will go to the king."

I know how Esther felt on the third day. I can imagine how it was when the morning dawned and she knew what a fearful thing she faced, knowing that she had to risk her life by entering the king's presence without his permission. I know how it was that she went anyway. Going in spite of her fear and buoyed by her faith: all that I can understand from my own life.

In my illustrated Bible, Esther is truly beautiful, and I do not doubt that the real queen was as well. It is, then, not so surprising that when she appeared before him, King Ahasuerus extended his scepter, which was the sign that she was welcome. Her courage saved the Jews. At Purim, this story is told in homes and temples around the world. When the name of the evil Haman is uttered, the people make a great hissing. That is my favorite part.

The beautiful Esther went in spite of her fear and was welcomed by her king. The little Mindy went, but I do not believe that I was welcomed at Heywood Avenue School. I do not believe that any of us who went felt wanted or beautiful. It is one thing to be deeply frightened and then triumphant. It is another to be so fearful but not succeed.

I lost my school, a place that had made me feel welcome, a place where I felt like hopping. It took no effort to move through space. If place is embodied in our bones, muscles, and minds, then Oakwood Avenue School was in me like a pocket rocket. I had to reconstitute myself at Heywood, an alien setting where I was allowed but not embraced. I hopped to Oakwood because that school empowered me, it gave me energy to dance and fly. I had to push myself to Heywood, the strength of my will pounding at my wish to stay at home.

All new settings, in my lexicon, became something to fear. To get there required a fight between will and wish. Each and every time, I had to battle this out. My will drew strength from my parents' values: the need to go was morally binding and hence nearly inescapable. I was a hero because I went, but no one knew just how much heroism it took to go and go and go.

That struggle did not end in the past. I still live with timidity and obstinacy warring in my bones. Go and die or stay and die. Every day is the third day. I usually go.

ADRIFT

The house was old, built perhaps in the 1890s, and had no acquaintance with insulation. It had a coal furnace which we all learned to manage, feeling like pioneers. It did provide even steady warmth, except in the coldest weather. We loved the house for reasons which were probably more romantic than practical. It had French doors, facing the street, which provided a charming view and bone-chilling drafts. It had a brass knocker representing a lady's bejeweled hand in an exotic style. We liked to think it might be Greek. It had a front staircase overlooking the parlor. The wall was papered with giant blue medallions tattered with age. We never could figure a way to repaper that wall, for it extended so high above the staircase with no place to set a ladder. So we lived with the medallions. At the back of the house a second staircase connected the kitchen with the second story, which had been servants' quarters. (The servants did not come with the house.) With two such staircases, it was almost our first thought that this would be a marvelous place to play hide-and-seek! I don't think we ever did, but it was that sort *of house.*

Frances (Crystal) Hale
Memoir, 1995

It had been snowing all day, and the ground was covered with maybe a foot of snow — a lot of snow, but the roads were still passable. The phone rang, with Sally Crystal, my best friend, asking if I wanted to go sledding on South Mountain Reservation. Her brothers, Steve and Roy, were home from college. They had sleds and a toboggan and the family car. The Crystals had a way of showing up at the drop of a hat, creating action and happiness. For years their parents, Dan and Fran, had led the merry band. But when Steve got a driver's license, the kids took over running the show. For me, the Crystals were a magic act, always up to something that was going to be fun.

I remember the sensation that night of my feet sinking into the snow on the hillside. It was one of my favorite spots since I had won a day camp hula hoop contest there: first prize in the "funniest" category for my imitation of Elvis Presley. That summer place seemed to be just under the bed of powder that was engulfing me. I remember laughing and throwing snowballs and making snow angels. We didn't laugh exactly the same way we had when we were kids, since we had all become conscious of love, sex, and gender. We were finding out who we would be to each other as men and women. The laughter grew out of all the years and was part present, part past, and part future. I don't remember who was there, or what happened. I didn't realize—one never does—that I should pay attention because it was all coming to an end.

The Crystals knew themselves to be "The Crystals." Their family identity was strong and charged. If my family never went anywhere together, their family went everywhere together. And where they went, it was fun to be. At least that was my perception. All families with an odd number of children are in need of another, and I was the "friend for Sally" who got to go along on the family adventures. I spent as many minutes of my life at their house as I could persuade my mother to allow. I went on summer vacations with them. I took lessons with them. I adored them.

Take Dan and Fran, for instance. Before they invented search engines on the Internet, there was Dan. Dan scoured junk shops, thrift shops, and used bookstores for "stuff" he brought home in boxes. He found skis, snowshoes, football equipment, thirty volumes of Alexander Dumas (*Man in the Iron Mask, Thirty Years Later*, etc.), ten volumes of Charles Dickens, toy Singer sewing machines, stuffed animals, records, and the dog. Their dog was named Loki, after the Nordic trickster god. The name was apt—not for the dog, who was kind and patient and never played a trick in her life—but because it symbolized the expectation of the unexpected that was characteristic of the Crystal household.

The stuff played an enormously important roles in our lives. The Crystal family home at 10 South Maple Avenue, like a Japanese tearoom, was a perfect setting for the ceremonies that went on there. A tearoom, in the classic design, is a ten-foot-square rustic hut, set in a formal garden, whose simplicity allows the mind to ponder the mysteries and wonder of the world. There is, maybe, one thing in a teahouse. The Crystal house on South Maple Avenue had boxes and boxes of things, and we found wonder by trying to imagine what to do with them. There seemed to be an inexhaustible supply of things for the four of us to explore.

But Dan, ostensibly shopping for us, was actually a bit of a pack rat, perhaps gathering "belongings" because he didn't quite "belong." As a kid watching the grown-ups, I knew that Dan wasn't considered "one of the guys" by the other dads. My dad was one of the guys, Mort Stavis was one of the guys, most of the other dads were "guys," but Dan wasn't. The "guys," for example, took their achievements for granted and rarely spoke of them; Dan talked on and on about the cases he had won or famous people he had met. It was awkward to see the other dads not quite include him. My mother would get a sad, frustrated look on her face as she watched this, though she never said anything. Nobody ever said anything, so I don't know why the men felt that way. But I know it was a weight on Dan that he could never shake. So he bought stuff. And he put his unhappiness on his kids: he expected Steve to be what he couldn't be, and he yelled at them all too much and not for "good" reasons. Not yelling over principles (which was, by my child's standards, more or less OK), but yelling because he had a hard day at work and didn't know how to metabolize his pain. Sure, you had a hard day at the office, but don't take it out on the kids, as the aspirin ads advised. I think now that he was yelling from deeper hurts and disappointments, but I don't know what they were. That nonbelonging made Dan very important to me. As a nonbelonger myself, I found a likeness in him that I hadn't located in many other adults.

Dan was also the guy you most wanted to have around on Christmas, because he discovered the absolutely best presents and there were always *boxes* and *boxes* of them. Though Dan was the guy you least wanted to have around when you wanted to be kid-silly after dinner, I secretly always took some comfort in watching Dan berate everybody as it made me think better of my own dysfunctional family. The Crystals probably took the same comfort from watching me.

Fran Crystal made the house. She is one of those people whose taste is unerring, which stood her in good stead as she tried out her ideas. She was a young mother and a nursery school teacher. She had somehow imbibed the free spirit of Isadora Duncan: she wanted music and dance and light and pattern to create rhythms, joy, and happiness for her family. I ask Fran who played the piano. "Well, I did, a little. But you have to have a piano in a house, in case somebody comes by who plays the piano and then they'll play for you. Anyway, I used it to learn folk songs. After I'd sounded it out, then we'd learn it. You know, there was a lot of dancing in the living room because if there was music, why, you were supposed to dance!" Isadora Duncan dancing, with scarves and ideas, more content than form. Feeling. Expression. What comes to mind when you hear this beat? And this one? Fran would pound her drum or strum her autoharp, and Sally and I would dance.

Fran was definitely a major mover and shaker among the women I knew, as well as my mother's best friend. She had a tendency to treat everyone as if they were children in her nursery school, an occupational hazard of sorts, but not a terrible character flaw. She managed the situation with Dan by trying to smooth things over. She was convinced that one ought to overcome adversity. She tried to keep the peace at whatever cost, mostly by stretching herself to patch things together, until she couldn't stretch anymore. In the 1950s, Dan, like my dad and a lot of other dads, was allowed to indulge his anger at the cost of other people. It wasn't physical battering, but the waves of unjustified anger hit us hard, nonetheless.

The hurting energy of the Crystals was sustained, contained, assuaged, revived by 10 South Maple Avenue, the house where they lived, allowing space for dancing and singing and reading and playing. "There was no grass in the middle of the yard," Fran remembers, "because there was always a football game going on. We were the only family on the block nutsy enough to let all the kids play football in the yard." And that is exactly why we flourished there.

My love for the Crystals' house is deep and pure and unambivalent. I went there to be happy, and I have never been in a place that so comforted me. The house was a modest Victorian, built in

East Orange in the late 1890s as the trolley suburbs were growing up around the cities. It occupied a wide and deep lot on a street full of big, comfortable houses. South Maple Avenue only really ran for one block, from Central Avenue to Main Street. The big shade trees that had been growing for seventy years kept the sidewalks cool and sheltered. On fall days, the crunch of leaves on the slate sidewalks filled me with deep and profound pleasure.

The house was set to the left and front of its lot. A short flight of stairs led up to a porch that ran the breadth of the house. It was a typical Victorian with tall windows on the first floor. As you entered the door, the front stairs rose on the left and the living room lay on the right. Through the living room was the dining room and beyond that the kitchen. Off the kitchen was a second porch with a picnic table for summer dining. A narrow set of stairs for the maid ran up from the kitchen to the second floor. At the top, just off the stairs, was the maid's room and next to that the huge bathroom, with a claw-foot tub. From there, a short rise of several steps led up to the master bedroom and the library. Between those two rooms were the stairs to the third floor, where there were two more rooms. Light poured in from windows everywhere. None of the house was dark. It was wide and high and open. Except the basement, which was dark and awful, much spookier than my basement. That was where the coal stove, the water heater, and the excess books were stored. But their furnace was Steve's job, not mine, so that was that.

Because you could run up the front stairs and down the back stairs, or up the back stairs and down the front stairs, or up to the third floor, or outside or around the house or around the block, activity simply flowed through the place. The house was energetic and nurturing. I never arrived there without immediately feeling that I wanted to be there.

Sally was the center of my universe. She was my hero. She was brilliant. She was a daredevil. She was wildly creative. We had things in common. What does a four-year old have in common with a three-year old? Who can remember how you know at that age that a friend is friend? But we did. Sally was my friend and my leader. She was always convincing me to do things I regretted. "Oh no," she says, "not the Hostess cupcake story again." Once we had a dime. She convinced me that something called a Hostess cupcake was the most amazing confection ever invented. Further, she said, we should walk barefoot around the corner to the store and buy one with our dime. She explained that she had been raised in the country and therefore had very tough feet that were made for walking on concrete in the middle of the New Jersey summer. She was very convincing. I wanted to eat this Hostess cupcake thing, and I wanted to have strong country feet.

It was a scorching hot day, and the concrete must have been over a hundred degrees. We nearly burned the soles of our feet on our way to the store. But we made it, and we spent our only dime on the Hostess cupcake. At first bite I knew I had been terribly deceived. This pink and white cardboard was not even something I could swallow. I was upset. "I remember the feeling of the hot sidewalk," she confesses these days.

She led me into many adventures. We tobogganed into a rosebush (she was an expert at driving and could avoid the bushes at the bottom of the hill), we invented a language to speak to each other (she used to speak other languages when she lived in the country and walked barefoot), we performed in talent shows (she was a great actress and dancer, and we were sure of winning). Sally was bold at making friends. Her opening gambit was "Have you read any good books lately?" This was excellent. It immediately eliminated all the nonreaders from further consideration and got the readers engaged with a favorite topic. Since Sally had read everything any little girl might have read, she was on solid ground to follow any lead. I was timid and had no accomplishments, so I watched with awe as she did these things.

Steve and Roy were Sally's brothers. I had a crush on Roy for a billion years. Every night that wasn't cloudy I wished on the first star that Roy would notice me. Steve was always in his room. He was brilliant, we knew, and disdainful of us. Time he had to spend with us he made sure we understood was a chore. Sally was the fastest reader I ever met and had read many of the classics by the time she was twelve. She was always using words she'd read but didn't know how to pronounce. My mother was very impressed by this, but Steve would always laugh at her and then the fighting would start and then Dan would yell, and then everyone would go to their rooms, etc. So Steve didn't mean much to me until he learned to drive. Steve reminds me that we all used to take baths together. The hot water heater, he remembers, was very old and not automatic. You had to turn it on to get hot water, and then there wasn't very much. He remembers that the house rule was that you couldn't have a bath by yourself, you had to share. This bath-taking was excellent fun but also a cause for a big fight over who got to take a bath with whom and then Dan would yell, etc.

When I ask various Crystals how we passed the time in those days, everyone has a different answer. Fran and Steve remember softball and football in the backyard—Fran because the games ruined the grass, Steve because he was always organizing these activities. Sally, of course, remembers what I remember: we played dolls. Sally's room was on the left as you came upstairs to the third floor. It was a big, wonderful room. She remembers that it had secret places, including one that allowed you to look out over the backyard without anyone in the yard seeing you. "I always imagined it was part of the Underground Railroad," she says. "I know the house wasn't built at the time of the Civil War, but you could have hid someone in the attic off my room." (I think of myself as the fugitive slave made safe by the house.) It had a big window where we once watched an eclipse of the moon. And it had a doll corner. There was no formal dollhouse, but rather a series of apple cartons painted in bright colors. "It was a series of rooms and dioramas," she says. "Do you remember the time we created a boat and took the Ginny dolls to sea?" I don't. Sally was always inventing some place for our Ginny dolls.

One of the greatest days of my life was the day I got my Ginny doll. Coming home on the bus from Newark, I begged my mother to let me get off at Sally's street and go to her house. She finally gave in. I ran breathless with joy down the street to the house and up to Sally's room. It was the culmination of a dream. Now we *both* had Ginny dolls. One of the worst days of my life was the day Sally got a Barbie and the second worst was the day she got Ken. Sexuality had reared its ugly head, and I wasn't ready for it. I felt terribly abandoned by my friend and never forgave Barbie for having such big breasts. In the days before Barbie, when we played with our Ginny dolls, we were able to create complete alternate worlds. Left to ourselves, in a quiet room, with hours to play together, we went far away from East Orange. We knew the way to Narnia then.

Fran's dreams of family involved getting everyone together, and that meant dinner. Dinner was always eaten in the kitchen. The dining room fulfilled a higher purpose as a storage unit. Pretty much anything you couldn't find was there, including the piano, which you couldn't find because so much stuff was piled atop it. I think the Crystals ate there on holidays, but I had holidays with my family and therefore cannot vouch for the fact that anyone ever ate in the dining room or played the piano.

The kitchen was a big kitchen with a pantry and lots of windows. "So many windows you couldn't put cabinets," Fran recalls. "It was the kind of house where things hadn't been planned, they'd happened and that made you think about what had gone before, who had lived there and how." The fireplace in the kitchen, which once held the stove, was one of those reminders of other times. Over the fireplace was painted the wish, "Give us bread and roses." The Crystals ate at a big round oak table. They used Stengleware plates. Stengle was a pottery factory in New Jersey that created a unique look by capturing folk art designs in solid, comforting ceramics. If you were poor, you could go to the factory store in Flemington and buy the remainders, and that was what Fran had done. Stengleware always created, for me, a sense of wonder. Dishes to dream by.

My mother, when asked what she remembers about 10 South Maple Avenue, always says, "baked potatoes." Fran apparently felt that this was a good food for children. She also liked to warm the plates for dinner. Sally and I, as girls, were recruited to participate in the work that went into preparing these eating rituals. Sally thought of this as "chores" and tried to avoid it. I thought of it as rustic and enchanting and was happy to help. At least that's how I remember it. I was not a chore enthusiast at home: this was away-from-home behavior. Dinner was a time for talking. The Crystals were always talking about or planning something. Sally was not the only adventurer in the lot. Fran encouraged all her kids to experiment. Steve was the leader, I believe, in the hockey rink project, designed to cover a flat area at the bottom of the yard with enough ice for skating. Roy was nice. He didn't yell or pout, and he wasn't mean to Sally and me. He helped us a lot. Occasionally he would share with us the brilliant things he was thinking in his own quiet way. You had to stay on your toes to have dinner with the Crystals.

Take, for example, *Catch-22*. All the Crystals read the book and loved it and made jokes about the main characters. Steve said that I was too young to understand it, but of course I read it anyway, trying to keep up. I didn't understand it at all, and it was most frustrating that he was right about me being too young.

After dinner was dishes, which meant Sally and me helping Fran. They had a double sink and a ritual for dishwashing that you scrubbed the dish, submerged it in the rinse sink, and then fished it out with the tongs because the rinse water was so hot. Then you dried it and put it away. While you were doing this, you could look out the window at the porch and the trees and the house next door and daydream about the things you'd rather be doing. The onerous part was that the boys were already off playing, and we could hear their shouts and laughter while we toiled away.

Working while men played was a bit the rule in those days, at the Crystals and at other houses. Sally—and therefore I—had, courtesy of Dan, an amazing collection of early edition children's literature. In a remarkable number of stories—*What Katy Did, Pollyanna,* and *Jack and Jill,* just to name a few—the girls fell and broke their backs, a tidy metaphor for the constraints placed on them to make them accept their place. Doing the dishes by the window and listening to laughter outside foreshadowed our fate. I vividly remember one camping trip we took to Stokes State Park. Roy was pouting because he wanted to go fishing, and Fran wanted him to wash the dishes. I offered to wash the dishes so that he could go. He sauntered off. I felt engulfed in Fran's sacrifice. This was what she was doing all the time to make peace and keep it going.

Sally tells me that near the end—just before her parents divorced—the family was driving somewhere, accompanied by the usual fussing and whining. Fran pulled the car over and screamed, "Stop it! Stop it! I can't do this any more." Sally remembers, "It was the scariest moment of my life."

I felt the tiniest flicker of Fran's pain that morning in Stokes State Park. It terrified me. I can't do this for love, I thought. I must do this for love, I thought, proud that I knew how to sacrifice.

Dan was frightened, angry, loving, and kind. Fran was creative, energetic, day-dreamy, and nursery-school make-nice. Their strategies for managing the surging emotions were limited. Dan wanted to yell. Fran wanted to smooth things over. This was a fragile and unstable compromise for the family. Their energy and creativity could not sustain the family, if the emotional balance was not right, and it wasn't. Sometimes, I felt like the mother of all of them. I wanted them all to calm down and get along. But I was six or eight and didn't really understand. I remember a lithograph Fran and Dan had hanging over their bed. It depicted a Russian wedding feast. At the center of the picture was a swan being brought to the table for the feast, dressed in all its feathers. At the end of the table was the blushing virgin and her adoring husband. Around the table were the rabble who had been invited to the party. It was a powerful and evocative picture. Many years later Roy made a copy of it for me. I used to stare at it for hours. What did it mean? It symbolized the Crystals for me, and I thought if I could decode the picture I could help them.

But of course I couldn't—I couldn't help myself, and I desperately needed them to be the Crystals and to live at 10 South Maple Avenue. In 1963, however, the East-West Freeway tore through East Orange. It was just an old suburb, and it was time to open up the new suburbs. Steve points out that South Maple Avenue housed poor black families: the whites had already fled the area to live in West Orange or South Orange or Maplewood. East Orange, voted one of the most livable cities in America before the highway went through, had come to the end of its usefulness for the white middle class. What they needed now was a road to take them quickly out of

Newark and home to the hills. Tearing down towns and destroying neighborhoods that stood in the way was of little consequence to those who saw themselves as speeding to the end of the line.

The East-West Freeway ate the Crystals' house one day. They moved out of 10 South Maple Avenue on August 19, 1963, just a week before the historic March on Washington led by Martin Luther King Jr. My mother, who helped with the packing, said she had never seen so much stuff. It was exhausting and painful. It seemed, at the time, that they would move to a grander house at Warrington Place and be even more the Crystals. But Fran couldn't do it anymore. It was the 1960s, and in the middle of the civil rights movement it occurred to her that she needn't salve her husband's temper anymore. She didn't say it that way to herself, then or now. It's my version, based on what I saw and felt as a kid hanging out and trying to have fun.

Fran and my mom were always making gardens, and part of their efforts involved going on drives to gather plants. We would, with great tenderness, dig out the plants, wrap their little roots in damp cloths or paper, and rush home to put them back into the ground. This procedure had a high mortality rate. The saddest of the little plants seemed to be losing life, as if it were draining out of them, as they turned from firm, feisty little things into limp and lifeless green puddles. Charles Elliott, the garden writer, has described eighteenth-century efforts to create instant gardens by relocating mature trees. One leading landscape architect of that era—Capability Brown— accomplished this by wrenching trees out of the ground with a giant lever. His contemporaries were skeptical of his results, however, because the trees often died, and "in cases of success, such trees for several years grow so slowly as to remind one of the 'stricken deer'." [1]

The wrenching effects of uprooting a tree by force parallel the effects of upheaval and transplantation on other living creatures, including people. The German word for wrenching plants out of the ground is *Entwurzeln*, a hard-to-pronounce word, but useful for thinking about the problems people encounter when they are forced to move.

Let me illustrate with the story of one of the best-studied disasters in U.S. history, the Buffalo Creek flood. Buffalo Creek runs through a mountain hollow, a narrow flatland between the steep sides of the mountains of West Virginia. The area was settled by coal miners and families who lived in a string of small hamlets scattered up and down the creek. These families, largely recruited from the nearby mountains to work in the mines, were part of a deeply connected community that made life possible and even good, despite its difficulties. This lifestyle was founded on caring and geographic stability of the people.

On February 26, 1972, at about eight in the morning, disaster struck. The dam holding mining wastes broke, sending 132 million gallons of sludge downward onto the towns sited along Buffalo Creek. Like a wall, a tidal wave, it took *everything in its path.* That became the title of a landmark book about the disaster, written by Kai T. Erikson.[2] Over two hours, the wall of destruction, fed by houses and schools and railroad tracks, swept down the creek until it joined the Guyandotte River. By that time it had lost some of its ferocity and momentum: it was merely a flood. In its wake, 4,000 of the 5,000 residents of the hollow were homeless, and 125 were dead. The task of going on with life began.

Before the flood, the residents of Buffalo Creek had been embedded in a narrow world, dominated by the dangers of working in the coal mine and the joys of living in the close comfort of neighbors and family. Erikson asked, "What's a neighbor?" and the answer was, "Well, when I went to my neighbor's house on Saturday or Sunday, if I wanted a cup of coffee I never waited until the lady of the house asked me. I just went into the dish cabinet and got me a cup of coffee or a glass of juice just like it was my own home. They come to my house, they done the same. See?"[3]

In the aftermath of the flood, the communities along Buffalo Creek faced trials and tribulations, but faced them without their neighbors. The disruption of community begun by the flood was unfortunately augmented by the relief efforts of the U.S. government, which sent emergency trailers to house the displaced. But rather than reestablishing the old order, they put people in houses wherever they happened to be. This meant that people were living with strangers, cut off from the essential networks that had shaped their lives. Erikson quoted one resident who summed it up:

> We did lose a community, and I mean it was a good community. Everybody was close, everybody knowed everybody. But now everybody is alone. They act like they're lost. They've lost their home and their way of life, the one they liked, the one they was used to. All the houses are gone, every one of them. The people are gone, scattered. You don't know who your neighbor is going to be. You can't go next door and talk. You can't do that no more, there's no next door. You can't laugh with friends. You can't do that no more, because there's no friends around to laugh with. That don't happen no more. There's nobody around to even holler at and say 'Hi,' and you can't help but miss that. You haven't got nobody to talk to. The people that is there are so busy trying to put back what they have lost.[4]

In this matrix of prolonged displacement, people suffered monumentally. Not just immediately after the flood, but decades later, some flood victims continued to suffer from anxiety, depression, and other problems.[5] To a large extent, the disaster was a test of each family and of its children. The family's ability to work together to handle the disaster left as much of an impression as did the disaster. Adults had to mobilize the larger unit of the family. If they accomplished this, then the children learned to do so, as well. If not, then the children internalized fear and disorientation. In the absence of a strong community, family strength was the essential element that allowed people to survive well.

When we consider the enormous emotional damage endured by the survivors of Buffalo Creek, it sheds new light on the biblical proposal that only Noah's family survived the flood. Families attempt to hold themselves together, but they do so as individual units, bereft of the sustaining fabric of community. Not all can manage this task. Arleen Ollie, whose story I mentioned in chapter 1, told me she was a young girl in Roanoke, Virginia, when urban renewal bulldozed her house. Her parents bought a new house but decided not to live there. Instead, they moved to Connecticut to work as live-in household help. Arleen was sent to live with relatives and became a vagabond, moving from house to house, essentially on her own. The transition defeated the capacity of the Ollie family to reformulate itself in a new house. The Crystals faced just such a crisis.

The Crystals were, for everyone who knew them, a collective being. My family was a loose confederation of individuals, but the Crystals were a unit. Much as the individuals were powerful individuals, they were unique in relationship to the whole. Each of them, in whatever way they chose, had to *be* a Crystal. Steve, commenting on the burden of this, says, "You couldn't just be an ordinary slob who didn't care about books or about culture. You had to achieve, you had to make your mark." To be a Crystal was to be something, but not something ordinary. Flanders and Swan's comedy album, *At the Drop of a Hat*, contains a song about a reluctant cannibal, who swears, "I shall never let another man pass my lips." He is brought back into the fold, however, when his father points out that saying you won't *eat* people is like saying you *fight* people. Junior, shocked, says, "Don't *fight* people? Ridiculous!" Sally and I practiced saying "ridiculous!" until we could do a perfect imitation of Flanders and Swan. Stretching the analogy as far as it can go, the Crystal tribe had its own rules, and reluctant members were always won back to the fold by the impossibility of being something else. "Being *ordinary?* Ridiculous!" might have been their motto. And they were in it together. Thirty years later, people who knew them as the Crystals link Fran and Dan and Steve and Roy and Sally as if a rupture had never happened.

But in uprooting them from 10 South Maple Avenue to Warrington Place, the foundation that held the family together sagged and collapsed. I was at camp when the Crystals moved. Two years later, in 1965, another letter to me at camp announced the news that Fran and Dan had decided to divorce. On the side, my mother had penciled in, "Don't share this with Sally, as she hasn't been told yet."

We all floundered, then, I think. The foundations of my world were shaken. Perhaps in a domino effect, it was after their family crumbled that my family crumbled. In my mind, that sweet house is still there. The freeway has so deformed the land that the street doesn't seem to exist anymore.

America has wrecked more towns with urban renewal and high-ways than could floods, but the results are the same as those from Buffalo Creek. The uprooting of hundreds of people contributed to the downfall of East Orange as a livable city. Steve sums it up suc-cinctly: "It was a good town. All through school—grammar school, junior high school, high school—I knew one guy who got in trouble. He was arrested for joy riding or something, and sent to the boys' detention facility. And these were poor people in our town." By the 1990s, East Orange was rated as "drug-infested" and "crime-ridden" by any measure one might choose. For Sally, the conclusion is, "I lost my hometown."

I go by South Maple Avenue from time to time and I try to deci-pher the landscape. It is disorienting to look at the street because it ends where it shouldn't. How can that be? Perhaps the house didn't fall. Perhaps it vanished into a different dimension, like Brigadoon, where it waits for us.

Sally once told me she was a witch and could make things appear and disappear. She didn't feel like it that day, but she could. I think that one day, at the drop of a hat, she will do that magic and the house will reappear.

In the meantime, Sally has become an artist and finds in her quilts a way to piece things together.

RESURRECTION

The quiet room was beside the door,
its stern simplicity bathed in sunlight.
She entered alone, this ritual a
private one after the years of sharing.
The heavy shoes, no longer to clatter
on her feet, were carefully unlaced
and laid beside the chair.
She lifted off the veil — she
would have hair again to bounce
singing on her shoulders.
The habit was slowly unbuttoned.
How would it feel to walk in the wind
without its flap around her legs?
and where the habit of restraint
it had taught her body?
The cotton dress for which she was
exchanging it seemed flimsy and revealing.
The change completed, quickly and efficiently
as she had learned to do all things,
she turned to the door. Sucking in
the feeling of the latch in her hand,
she stepped forward into a world without walls.
The breezes tickled her ears
as they caught the sound of the
door locking behind her.

Mindy Thompson
"The Nun's Story," 1981

The first concrete action in medical school is finding a seat. On the opening day of medical school at Columbia University College of Physicians and Surgeons (P&S) in 1974, I entered PH 8/9 on the eastern side and chose a seat about three rows from the back in the side section. The rows were made of metal, with wooden backs and seats that folded down. The seats curved in a semicircle about the room, facing the multilayer blackboard. Our classroom extended through two floors of the building. From where I was located, it was a long shot down to the speakers' pit. Surrounded by the hundred and fifty members of my class, as well as the fifty or so first-year dental students, I was happy and confident. I had arrived.

Only a few days later a crisis shook my joy. Our first exam was scheduled on a Jewish holiday. Jewish holidays are taken for granted in New York. Jewish culture is so much a part of city life that alternate side of the street parking is suspended and schools are closed. A student raised his hand. "Can the exam be rescheduled?" he asked. I'm sure he was confident, as I was at that moment, that what he was asking was a trivial request.

The professor, with his gray hair and white coat, looked around, fixing us with a chilling stare. "If there are students in this class who have trouble with that date, perhaps they should have gone to another medical school in this city."

"Another medical school" meant Mt. Sinai or Albert Einstein, both founded to serve Jewish students excluded by quota systems from Columbia and like places. "Another medical school" meant "You don't belong here if you're Jewish." I hadn't thought about the Presbyterian Hospital in the City of New York as a religious entity until that moment.

Like a hairline fracture in a china cup, that moment disfigured my dreams of medicine. In some profound way, I was not prepared for my doctor heroes to be anti-Semitic. Whatever the faults of my college, they were largely problems of omission, not commission. I trembled in my seat, high up on the east side. I can remember feeling very alone. Would anyone help me fight this?

That moment of aloneness was very long. I wanted only to be a doctor, just like them. But just like *him?*

After class, milling around in the hall, I searched for David Himmelstein. I hadn't really gotten to know David before that day, but it was obvious that, if anyone was going to do something, it would be he. If hair and clothes were any marker, David was his own man. In a culture of button-down shirts, buzz cuts, and shiny wingtip shoes, David sported patchwork pants, a ponytail, and track shoes.

David asked me, "What did you expect? Who do you think they are?" I couldn't answer. I thought doctors were all good, like Dr. Alexander. I shook off David's questions. I didn't want to wonder about the entire foundation of the system: I simply wanted to protest one isolated, mistaken thing.

We did protest, the first of many reform efforts classmates and I made, with minimal success in altering the environment of the medical school and hospital. The protest did mark the start of an intense and important friendship with David.

David had consciously created a distance between the school and himself. Because his father was one of the surgeons who had founded the open-heart surgery group at Columbia and his mother was a leading child psychiatrist, David could not step entirely outside the profession. Furthermore, he was, even then, a doctor by nature and understanding, and his devotion to the practice of medicine was profound. He once rejected the idea taking a year off because, he concluded, "I'd never catch up on all the journal articles."

But David was not naïve. He accepted, even if I did not, that the medical profession actively participated in the creation and maintenance of the oppression of women, segregation by race, and discrimination by ethnicity and religion. He came to medical school knowing the system. He flaunted his difference as a way of being within the system, without buying into it. I thought it was weird, as did most of our classmates, but I was drawn to him because he wasn't afraid.

You couldn't be a halfway friend with David—it was in or out. He had, in essence, rejected the class. To be his friend entailed joining him in this stance. Although I thought his position was extreme—perhaps even unfounded—I changed to a seat next to his: the seat closest to the door on the west side of the amphitheater.

After that, medical school fell into a routine. The day began with a walk from my apartment at 185th Street down Fort Washington Avenue to 169th. At that point, I had to make a key decision: coffee and a roll from the Greek deli that used Greek diner cups or coffee and a donut from Chock Full O'Nuts in the Black Building (named after William Black, head of Chock Full O'Nuts). The Greek diner had been my choice for the two years before medical school. The Chock Full O'Nuts was a hole in the wall directly on the way to the amphitheater. I really liked the guy who ran it, and the coffee was good. Such major decisions about food occupied much of my little spare time in medical school.

Nourishment in hand, I headed for PH 8/9, where we sat from 9 A.M. to 5 P.M., Monday through Friday, listening to lectures. Every course began with a lecture on the cell wall, which had just been deciphered. Our professors loved to talk about it. It is one of the few things I truly mastered. Most of the time I had no idea what they were talking about, and my notes reflected my profound, complete confusion. This was especially true when they talked about submicroscopic processes. At the point at which you couldn't see it—and therefore had to take their word for it—I was in trouble. Electrolytes, for example, were new to me. I hadn't heard about electrolytes from Mr. Amen, my high school biology teacher, and I hadn't heard about electrolytes in college. Did these things really float around in the blood? I wasn't sure, and I wasn't eager to trust my professors. Anti-Semitism was new to me, and so were electrolytes. I put them in the same bag, one labeled "Caution—handle with care."

Pathology was an exception. In those days, pathology told the story of disease. David and I started going to the morning pathology rounds where the autopsies performed the previous night were presented. They served good coffee and let you look at things like lungs, blackened by cigarette smoke and filled with cancer.

These sessions were known as "Man in the Pan." The title was quite literal: the body parts were displayed in stainless steel bowls. Though I had great dismay and even revulsion in anatomy class, I found Man in the Pan riveting. We learned there the story of a person's life. It was a time to ponder the ends that had their beginnings in events far in the past. We were there to witness the mysteries of life and death: I liked that.

Even counting Man in the Pan, life was pretty dreary. To ease the boredom of our routine, we played a lot that year. After class, we would go to David's apartment on Riverside Drive. David would say, "Let's eat." Then he would make tuna salad.

David's Tuna Salad

tuna fish from a can
mayonnaise
apples
oranges
raisins
celery
anything else that might be good

After we ate the tuna fish salad, David would ask, "Want some brownies?"

David's Brownies

Melt together ⅓ cup butter and 2 squares bitter chocolate.
Mix together 1 teaspoon vanilla, ½ cup flour, 1 cup sugar, and 2 eggs.
Stir the two mixes together.
Put the mix in a pan and bake at 350° for 15–18 minutes.

Then David would ask, "Want to go to the gym?" We would climb into his Alfa Romeo and go to the gym at Columbia's 116th Street campus. Or he would ask, "Want to do carpentry?" We would go off to the lumber mill to buy fine hardwoods. I still work on a butcher block table of mahogany and maple that I made under David's direction.

We didn't always play; sometimes we were sad. I was far from over either the rigors of my childhood or my father's death. My marriage was floundering, my self-esteem rocky. David, having lost his dad at an even younger age than I had, harbored sorrows and confusion of his own. At such moments, we kept vigil over each other's grief.

The demands of school were never far from our minds, and foremost among them passing tests. David studied by flipping through the pages of a book while watching the Knicks. This didn't work for me: I studied a lot, but not very effectively. As David floated through racking up honors, I was having more and more trouble.

P&S in those days had a practice of sending letters announcing that you weren't doing well. You would get these letters at your school mailbox. The letters were curt and hurtful. Each time I got one I had to fight back tears. Tony, who ran the mailroom, watched these scenes with great concern. He didn't flutter, he didn't dash in to help. He would simply stand there, his blue eyes brimming with support, trying to give me enough strength to walk down the halls. I would stand, sometimes for many minutes, fighting for composure. Tony always waited with me until the waves of shock had passed.

My worst troubles were with anatomy. I was assigned to dissect the corpse of an elderly black woman who had died unattended. Her emaciated remains were frozen in a fetal position. She was too much like the grandmother I never had for me to cut into her. But it wasn't just the cutting—it was making sense of it all. Anatomy requires that the student develop a mental representation of the human body. For those of us who are not quick at such visual processing, this requires hours and hours of looking, drawing, examining, memorizing. I didn't understand the task or how to accomplish it. Faculty weren't telling, either, since they cherished a set of sadistic traditions centered around withholding guidance. Far from offering sympathy or support, they reminded us that what we faced was a piece of cake compared to what they had experienced as students.

My efforts at survival in medical school created an unstable situation that worsened before it got better. David was in love with an incredibly beautiful but hopelessly inaccessible woman. One day, in a moment of the truly remarkable insensitivity of which I am capable, I told him he should just forget her. David was so incensed that he stopped speaking to me.

At first, I was angry with him, and then it was summer vacation, so it didn't matter. Then it was school again, and that was awkward because we had planned our lives together. We were tethered in an awful incommunicado. And then there was the amphitheater. I still sat next to David every day. I couldn't move. That was my place, my seat in the scheme of things. My seat away from the anti-Semitism that I couldn't understand, and my seat with my friend. Except that my one friend wasn't speaking to me.

But then things really got worse. We entered a phase in which we had exams every week for ten weeks. The letters, the crying in front of Tony, and the fear got out of control. I didn't know what to do. Three people came to my rescue. First, Martha Stittelman decided to be my friend and moved her seat next to mine in the rafters. Maybe David wasn't talking to me, but I wasn't alone. Martha also cooked. Lentil soup and homemade bread. I expanded my cooking repertoire.

Martha's Lentil Soup

1 bag lentils
2 chopped onions
4 big carrots, maybe a little celery
salt and pepper
Place ingredients in a large heavy pot, fill pot with water, and
    simmer slowly for several hours until everything is soupy.

Second, Leslie Davidson helped me move my seat, transferring to the liberal section, five or six students who sat together in the middle of the amphitheater, a few rows down from the top. Leaving David felt awful, and for years — that is, until we started to talk again — I carried an aching grief for my lost friend.

Finally, there was Norman Kahn.

He was the head of our pharmacology course. He called me in because I hadn't done well on the exams. His small office in the Black Building was crowded. I sat on a rolling, squeaking chair facing him. "You don't know what's going on, do you?" he asked in his kindly fashion that conveyed respect and even affection for students. I felt, suddenly, relief and hope. I started to cry.

"I'm trying really hard," I choked out, between sobs, "but nothing's working." Boo hoo, boo hoo.

"Don't worry," he said. "I can help."

And that's when he told me the secret of medical school.

In the weeks that followed, I soared from poor-to-middling to the top of the class. I became an overnight success. No more letters, no

of Presbyterian, while the rich, white patients enjoyed the comforts of Harkness Pavilion. Nothing mattered to the business of the hospital except the bottom line.

I knew these things. I did not connect *being* a doctor to participating in the *business* of the hospital. In *The Lion, the Witch and the Wardrobe,* the classic tale by C. S. Lewis, four children, Peter, Susan, Edmund, and Lucy, are sent off to the country to escape the bombing of London.[1] They find themselves in a strange house belonging to an elderly professor. The professor has in his spare room a wardrobe full of old fur coats. As it turns out, the back of the professor's wardrobe opens onto an alternate world called Narnia. In the course of the story, first Lucy, then Edmund, then all four children find themselves there. The children are surprised by Narnia, but Narnia is expecting them because it is ordained that evil will be defeated when the Sons of Adam and the Daughters of Eve sit on the Thrones of Cairn. But, before that can happen, any number of problems must be resolved, not least of which is the treachery of Edmund.

Edmund gets into trouble because he is bewitched by enchanted Turkish Delights offered to him by the Wicked Witch. Thinking only of the candy, he betrays friends and family alike. It is only when he sees that the Witch is not his friend that he slowly comes to understand what he has done. I, too, had to overcome my enchantment before I could connect multiple realities.

ENCHANTED CANDY

While I was a secretary, I walked around the hospital in the uniform of my caste, a long blue coat. As a secretary, I was beneath the practical nurses, who were beneath the nurses, who were beneath the medical students, who were beneath the residents, who were beneath the doctors, who were beneath the chairmen, who were beneath the Great Men, who themselves were getting kind of close to God (or at least Godliness). In the halls and the cafeteria, the movements of the doctors dominated the space and the airways. "Paging Dr. X. Dr. X., please call extension 1-2-3," they repeated insistently. I longed to climb the ladder of success, to be a doctor.

My images of doctors were largely formed by the men who had

cared for my family and me in Orange, New Jersey. Most prominent of these was John Alexander, my father's good friend and my
pediatrician. I often had infectious conditions and high fevers when
I was a child. I can still see his calm face and hear his decisive voice.
"Cough," he would say, cutting through the haze of fever. I would
cough. He would move his cold stethoscope. "Cough again."

I would protest. "It hurts too much."

"Cough," he would insist. I would cough. Then he would go away
and my mother would shovel medicine down my throat, and I would
start to mend. His face, viewed through my delirium, was the face of
medicine.

I decided, sitting in my little office in Maxwell Hall, watching the
ice float by, that I would go to medical school. I immersed myself in
premed courses at City College and then at Columbia University's
School of General Studies. I found myself in the world of premeds,
which is to say, in the world of people transfixed by their dream of
doctoring.

It is a bizarre kind of stupor. It seems, from the perspective of
the premed, that the only career of any value is medicine. Everything
hinges on getting into medical school. Therefore, getting up in the
morning and going to bed at night and every moment between are
consecrated to achieving this goal. It was not a part of that state of
wanting to think that medicine, itself, had defects or deficits. When
I entered a graduate program in nutrition at P&S, the idealization
intensified. There we were cheered on by Myron Winnick, a pediatrician who envisioned making doctors more aware of diet by seed-
ing the profession with people trained in nutrition. "Go," he told us.
"Go to medical school." How we hungered to do just that!

The fact that it was extremely hard to get into medical school only
served to whet our appetites. MCAT scores and recommendations, A's
in key courses and dazzling essays, figuring out how many schools to
apply to and then filling out endless applications: these things filled
our days and nights. Counsel that urged prudence was brushed aside.
I remember a kind letter from H. Ronald Rouse, national director
of the Woodrow Wilson National Fellowship Foundation. He worried that I had left Yale because I found it inhospitable to women

and minorities. Medicine, he pointed out, did not have a good reputation in that regard, and I might be disappointed again. Impossible, I thought to myself. Medicine is wonderful.

REAL LIFE

Thus, in the real life of my days, I had great trouble acknowledging that the business machine of Presbyterian had anything to do with doctoring. Doctoring was pure, I wanted to believe. It was hard to connect the evils that I saw with the art that I wanted to practice. Events in my second year of medical school provided perspective.

The basic course in psychiatry divided the class into small groups. David and I had joined the group entitled the Psychiatry of Racism and Poverty, led by Bruce Ballard, the only African-American psychiatrist at the hospital. One part of the class session each week was devoted to interviewing hospitalized patients. Another part was devoted to the creation and presentation of a group project.

While carrying out the interviewing portion of our course, we noticed that we had encountered only white patients. When we asked why this was, we were told that most of the patients we interviewed came from the fifth-floor treatment unit at the Psychiatric Institute (PI), where there were few black or Hispanic patients. We were well aware of the segregation at Presbyterian Hospital, and it seemed likely what we were encountering at PI was another example of that. We took on the challenge of examining the ways in which race structured life at PI.

The data were clear and damning. There were, at the time, two main treatment services. One unit, on the sixth floor, served the "community" and was open to those who lived in the area, including people of color. The other, on the fifth floor, was a research unit that accepted patients according to strict criteria or political pull. The patient population was 68 percent black and Hispanic on PI 6, but 98 percent white on PI 5. I still shiver to remember what a staff person told us: "We couldn't admit blacks to PI 5. All of our patients have to be highly intelligent, IQ of 130 or more." The distribution of blacks and Hispanics among staff was also sharply skewed, with a preponderance of minorities in housekeeping and other nonskilled positions but hardly any among the physicians who ran the hospital.

Such explosive information was painful for us. And there was more where that came from. That summer, two medical students, Nancy Anderson and Mary Roman, prepared a report on the status of minority and women students at P&S.[2] They made a thorough investigation of the process of desegregation, which had been under way for several years as part of the nationwide drive toward desegregation in medical education. At P&S, the increase in admission of minority students was not accompanied by any efforts to help minority students adjust. There was little support and no organized tutoring. Failures were frequent and emotionally devastating to the whole group: one student had to repeat the first year in 1971, three in 1972, five in 1973, and one in 1974.

While the faculty thought of the students as underprepared, from the perspective of many of the students—and this was certainly my experience—racism at P&S made it difficult to function on a day-to-day basis. One student was quoted in the report as saying that

I expected it to be a lot like undergraduate—undergraduate had its problems, but I didn't think there would be any more [here]. . . . Here, the minority, and especially the black, students are running into what people ran into in colleges ten or twenty years ago. . . . It's a funny feeling to realize that you may not be accepted because of color.[3]

Rereading the report from the vantage point of twenty years, I am reminded of a peculiar aspect of the experience of medical school, which was the frequent and unexpected displays of racism and sexism. Just as the anti-Semitism displayed in the first weeks of school was stunning to me, so were any number of remarks about minorities and women. The paradigmatic story was that of a noted neurologist who insisted to a group of students and house officers that "the colored race" had the "worst drinking problem." One woman, quoted in the Anderson-Roman report, described her first year of medical school as if she were at war: "My experience at medical school can only be likened to a foray into an enemy camp. The academic environment is dehumanizing and even Kafkaesque."[4]

It was typical of the environment at P&S that the attacks were not personal: Dr. Merritt and other old-timers were masters of the courtly style. None of them ever made a racist remark about me to my face. But, as a black student, I was caught in the net of association that went something like this: black patients were drunkards and should be segregated in certain parts of the hospital; black students were inferior, and therefore black doctors had no place in the hierarchy at P&S.[5]

We students managed this onslaught by equivocating. We did not hesitate to point out what we saw as wrong, but we usually cloaked our criticisms in conciliatory language. For example, when my psychiatry group presented its findings, we hastened to reassure the audience that no person was responsible for what we had seen. Our report notes,

> In presenting this discussion, we did not intend to make any indictments. We merely wanted to make people aware of a situation that they may not have realized existed. If in fact there is institutional racism at PI we feel that it probably is unintentional. If we can make people think about effecting changes, then we will have accomplished our purposes.[6]

Such half-stepping was a way of being comfortable when confronted with a distressing reality. There were simple bits of joy to be had in medical school, and it became more and more my custom to grab them. I remember, as if it were yesterday, spending a Sunday with Martha studying on the second floor of the Black Building. Microwaves had just been installed in one of the cafeterias. We took a lunch break and walked over to the supermarket on Broadway. We studied the frozen foods for a long time before deciding on broccoli au gratin. We took it back, heated it in the microwave, and savored each hot and tasty morsel. When the meal was done, we headed back to studying, six hours of uninterrupted work looming ahead, but greatly comforted because we had had our meal.

I was to discover that I had come to value comfort above all else. I learned this in a way that is still painful to recall. In the last part of the second year, school was taken over by planning for third-year clerkships. Everyone had to complete six-week blocks of surgery, surgical subspecialties, medicine, pediatrics, neurology, psychiatry, and ob-gyn, but we couldn't all do it in the same order or at the same hospitals. In our world of few choices, the selection of the order of the clerkships and the hospitals loomed large.

The first step in this process was the organization of rotation groups that would move from specialty to specialty together, but subdivided among a given number of hospitals. The choice of hospital depended on one's lottery number. Martha and I were in the same rotation group, but I had a good number and she had a bad one. Bad numbers usually meant Harlem Hospital, dreaded by most medical students because it combined the worst living conditions with the most drudgery. For some, the downside of Harlem was alleviated by its service to poor African Americans. This fact failed to comfort me, accustomed as I was to Orange Memorial and other hometown hospitals that managed to serve poor black people without exposing them to wretched conditions. It didn't comfort Martha, either, and she dreaded the day on which we made our choices.

Our group met in a small classroom facing Fort Washington Avenue. We gathered around the blackboard and laid out the possibilities, so many to St. Luke's, so many to Presbyterian, and on and on. Then the selection began. The first few rounds were easy. It was the medicine rotation away from Presbyterian Hospital that did me in. "Mindy, where do you want to go for Medicine?" the leader asked.

I meant to say, "Harlem."

Instead, I said, "St. Luke's," much to my own consternation choosing comfort over friendship. I left Martha to go to Harlem by herself. This is the friend who sat by me when I sat by David, who wasn't speaking to me. This is the friend who made me bread and lentil soup.

"Get over it," Molly advises me more than twenty years later. "Call her up and tell her to get mad at you. Then you can justify yourself, and it will be all right."

What she is saying has merit, but I know, in my heart of hearts, that I sold out my friend for enchanted candy. I passed an intensely lonely rotation at St. Luke's, but it was clean and warm. I do call Martha, though. She doesn't remember my abandonment or hold it against me. "I'm glad I went to Harlem," she says. "It taught me that less is less, and inadequately funded services for the poor are simply bad medicine."

WITNESSING

In those days I was like Edmund hungering for candy, but I was also like Peter, trying to be brave in attacking the inhumanity of the place, and like Susan, calling for help when I was floundering, and finally, like Lucy, witnessing the ebb and flow of the life force.

After the third-year rotations were over, I had a chance to escape the hustle and bustle of the medical center. Oddly enough, it was David's mother, Eleanor Galenson, who gave me the opportunity to participate in a research project studying deaf infants. I spent many hours behind a one-way mirror watching a little boy with very little hearing learn about the world. It was not nirvana for me, this little research world at the Lexington School for the Deaf. I was troubled by the strange contradiction of not letting deaf children employ sign language. But watching Alan find his way was another matter. Even at this remove, my notes create a scene that I remember well. Alan and his mother, Cynthia, had arrived late, after a hearing aid test. He was a little cranky due to a bout of diarrhea. The following excerpt charted five minutes of nursery school on April 5, 1978; the bullets mark thirty seconds of elapsed time.

· Alan runs to the bed, jumps up and down on the bed, over to table where paint things are out. Cynthia goes to get coffee. Warren [the other staff member assigned to work with Alan] puts apron on A., dips A.'s finger in paint. A. vocalizing. Distressed face.

· Gets out of chair, over to mother. She brings him back to table and encourages him to paint. He picks up brush, bangs on egg cartons. "Bababa . . ."

· Looking for mom. Runs over to where she is sitting on sofa. "You want [smock] off?"

· She takes it off. He rides "Giddy up."

· He stands quietly near her, looking around. Reaches for toy, looks at David [another child] in crib. Cynthia kisses the top of his head. He sits on her lap. She kisses him again.

1. Ernie Thompson, as he often looked
in the years in retreat. ca. mid 1950s–
early 1960s.

2. Dr. John Alexander, president of the board of education, at the microphone arguing that the Orange City Council approve funds for the new high school. August 1968.

3. The Thompson family. Mindy on the left, Maggie holding Josh. 1956.

4. The Crystal family celebrating
Sally's birthday. From left: Steve, Fran,
Dan, Sally, and Roy. September 1955.

5. Mindy Thompson's kindergarten
picture. 1955–56.

6. The Kaufman/Fullilove family in 1985.
From left: Bob Fullilove, Dina
Kaufman, Mindy Fullilove (at bot-
tom), Bobby Fullilove, Molly
Kaufman, and Kenny Kaufman.

7. Maggie Thompson and Bob Fullilove
in the garden of the thin house. 1993.

· He stands on her lap. "Bababa . . ." then sits down again.

· He pulls her hand "eee" ("come" sound). "I'm drinking my coffee." He gets up, she follows. He sees Warren, takes cracker. Emily [staff member] cleaning table for snack.

· Alan climbs into chair. Mother goes to get crackers for him. She goes over by mother's group, but he runs after her, brings her back.

· Children gather at table for snack. Alan waiting for drink, claps hands and says baba. He gestures, "Open, shut them" [hand motions that accompany a favorite snack-time song]. They begin to sing.

· Cynthia walks around table to be facing Alan. He follows and clings to her. Sits in chair. She walks off. He looks all around for her, distressed. She comes back with Ernie [Sesame Street puppet]. He chortles as Ernie taps his head.

· Warren puts Ernie on hand, Alan puts hand in puppet's mouth.

Over the weeks, such detailed notes built a picture of a mother who was not quite fully available for her baby and of her son's very active efforts to keep her with him. The staff of the nursery worked hard to support Cynthia and Alan. For Cynthia, a deaf son was a tragedy, and she was not done with her mourning. Why had it made her so sad? I didn't know the answer. I knew that it needn't hurt like that, because I often watched a deaf couple who brought their youngster to the nursery. The baby's deafness was not the problem in that instance: rather, communicating with the hearing world challenged them.

I whiled away the last few months of medical school watching Alan grow and Cynthia mourn. Lucy, in Narnia, is gifted with a magic potion that heals the injured. As the first injured soul she has treated begins to revive, she sits in fascination, watching his revival. The Lion chides her to hurry away and heal others who are injured. There is always that voice, urging one on to another healing. But I, for one, gradually came to feel that there was nothing more fulfilling than the opportunity to watch the healing unfurl.

DEEP MAGIC AND DEEPER MAGIC

When Lucy first arrived in Narnia, she stumbled into Mr. Tumnus. She explained to him that she had come through the back of the wardrobe in the Professor's spare room. The sense Mr. Tumnus makes of this is that she had just come from the bright city of War Drobe in the land of Spare Oom. Of course, I wasn't Lucy—or Peter, or Susan, or even Edmund—I was just myself trying to figure out the strange world into which I had stumbled.

That strange world made demands on me to be brave, honest, caring, and questioning in ways that I had never experienced before. I had to reconcile my view of doctoring with my new understanding of the business of medicine. Many settings make no such demands. My job as a secretary, for example, asked little more of me than that I tolerate a lot of boredom. I didn't have to be brave to be a secretary; I only had to arrive on time and answer the phones politely. If my vision was inadequate to my new world, my emotional equilibrium was even more precarious. Then I discovered the *deeper* magic.

The *deep* magic of Narnia demands that traitors be put to death. But the *deeper* magic decrees that a willing sacrifice will live again. Because of the deeper magic, the Lion can die for Edmund, the traitor, and yet live again.

Death confronted me in such a way my third year of psychiatric residency. At that point in my training I was learning to manage the care of outpatients, that is, people who came in for regular office visits, rather than the hospitalized patients I had attended up until then. By January, I had collected twenty or so patients, of whom six were struggling to find the will to live. It seemed that I talked about life and death from early morning until late at night. I fought the suicidal ideas of others with all my will, and every bit of ground I gained with them forced me to ask myself: what am *I* living for? As I fought for life, I became more and more aware of my own confusion and emptiness.

Then, abruptly, it all shifted. I met a man who was very close to death, having, it seemed to me, lost the thread of life, the umbilical cord that keeps us breathing. I was deeply frightened for him, partly because of his illness and partly because he was a wonderful person and I couldn't bear the thought of losing him. A few days after I first met him, he made a suicide attempt but stopped himself. He agreed to enter the hospital, where I hoped he would be safe. For some weeks, the report was that he seemed to be getting better, and slowly the constant observation, a precaution that surrounds vulnerable patients to keep them from hurting themselves, was removed. I can only guess that it was in a wave of renewed despair that he chose to end his life. The chief resident called me to tell me of the tragedy. His voice was profoundly comforting, reaching through the shock and terror of the news to ground me. Although I had known that patient for only a few days, I felt that I had lost a dear friend. I grieved for his loss, I grieved for the love of life that had been extinguished within him, I grieved for my own harried soul.

In the profound tragedy of my patient's death, I understood something about the fiber of life. I knew that I, too, might choose death if I did not find my way to life. It was time to decide. However many pushes and pulls, however much terror and desire, I had to decide what kind of life I wanted to live, what kind of doctor I wanted to be, what kind of person I was. Enough with Susan/Edmund/Peter/Lucy: who was *Mindy?*

I am sure that I was finally able to ask such a question because of the strong support I received from my teacher, Estelle Schecter. I said to Estelle one day that my insides felt like the *Star Wars* scene in which Princess Leia and the gang fall into a mucky garbage pit in which lurked slimy, tentacled creatures. She sent me, the next day, a drawing of planks over the muck with a little flower peeping through. Oh, I thought, I can rearrange this internal swamp. I hadn't thought of my insides as malleable or movable. She sent a second drawing of planks and flowers and music to soothe the savage beast. Oh, even more wonder, I realized, I could have joy in my life.

Some of my first decisions were frivolous. I decided I was a person with long hair. I decided I was not a fat person. Later decisions were more profound. They involved finding ways to be a doctor within the business of medicine. I could, at last, answer David's question. I could admit who doctors were. I knew what they were doing. More importantly, I knew what I was doing, and how I wanted to be a doctor. Here is my credo:

I believe in the sanctity of the human spirit.

I believe in the creation of health, rather than the treatment of disease.

I believe that health care is a right, not a privilege.

I believe that the business of medicine cannot snuff out the deeper magic of doctoring.

I believe in the healing power of that deeper magic.

I believe in being a witness to rebirth.

I believe that medical care must be delivered in places that are open, respectful, and welcoming of all who need healing. The deeper magic cannot flourish under conditions of segregation. Splits in the soul, splits in the organization of place, must be brought together to create a whole that is larger than the sum of its parts.

IMMERSION

4-5-89/8:32 A.M.

Writing in the hotel on Day 2 of our visit. So far the trip has exceeded, by a great deal, my expectations. We've had (or should I say, I've had) any number of opportunities to work on my French: (1) the taxi into town was great. A Cambodian driver (très sympa) was perfectly happy to 'causer un peu' with me about speaking French; (2) the shopping expedition to les Galeries Lafayette was a challenge of the 'première ordre', lots of discussion about what to get; (3) FRENCH TV!! Given the variety one hears of this language in a range of situations, from news broadcasts to game shows to soaps, I am getting better and better at hearing the language and adding to my vocab . . .

Bob Fullilove
family trip diary, 1989

In 1964, I was thirteen. I spent half the summer in Bermuda, walking on the beaches, and half the summer in Maine, paddling the Blodgetts' lake. I had not yet met my husband-to-be, Bob Fullilove, who was then twenty, spending the summer in Mississippi as a civil rights worker engaged with the Student Nonviolent Coordinating Committee (SNCC), called "Snick" for short, in a voter registration campaign. The iconic image of that time, in my mind, is that of fire hoses turned on black protesters. The image that keeps reappearing in books and magazines, however, is that of a group of young people, black and white, arms crisscrossed, holding hands beside a bus, as they readied to go to the South, and singing "We Shall Overcome."[1] Bob is the black guy on the left in the picture. In some shots, if you look closely, you can read "Fullilove" on his badge.

Bob says it really wasn't the summer of fire hoses: that was the summer before in Birmingham. But people had seen the hoses and been horrified, as was I. The vision had two parts: not only the indignity, the outrage of fire hoses turned against fellow human beings, but also the courage and humanity of the crouched but undaunted protesters, putting their bodies on the line for freedom. It was a magnetic image. One could not simply see such pictures, one had to respond to them.

Some visions do call men and women to action. Tennyson, in his famous poem, *Idylls of the King*, relates the story of the knights of the Round Table so overcome by a vision of the Holy Grail, shrouded in a cloud, that they swore to search until they had seen it clearly. King Arthur was saddened when he heard this, perhaps because he understood or had a premonition that such a vision, such a call, was the beginning of a transformation of the Self. "But one hath seen, and all the blind will see," he said. "Go, since your vows are sacred, being made. . . . Many of you, yea most, return no more: ye think I show myself too dark a prophet."[2]

Perhaps that same dread explains the reaction of Bob's mother to his summer plans. He remembers that she was hysterical at the idea. It made her crazy to think about it. But his father gave him a thousand dollars and said "Go." His father was optimistic and proud of Bob for daring. Bob, like all the others soon scheduled to head to Mississippi, wondered if he would make it back alive. In fact, as he made the round of good-byes in New Jersey, it was plain that many people considered him lost. Young men too afraid to go shook his hand with respect. Women looked at him with wonder. He was terrified.

The terrors, though different from those in Birmingham, were very real. Days after the first wave of volunteers arrived in Mississippi, three of them, Andrew Goodman, Michael Schwerner, and James Chaney, were kidnapped. Their murdered bodies were found later in the summer. By the time the summer was over, four people had been murdered, four people critically injured, thirty black homes or businesses bombed or burned, thirty-seven churches burned or bombed, eighty people beaten, and a thousand people arrested. The fear was broader and deeper and wider than the simple numbers reveal. The volunteers were going into the last bastion of segregation to challenge White Supremacy. The Reign of Terror, by which White

Supremacy had ruled for hundreds of years, was turned against them. They were stalked, harassed, threatened, intimidated, belittled, degraded. It was a summer of learning to manage fear.

Arriving at the orientation in Miami, Ohio, Bob wanted more than anything to fit in with the staff. In the small world of SNCC, the staff, those young people who worked full-time for The Movement, had dared the highways and back roads of the South. Each time they drove into a small town, they showed that it could be done. Each time they drove back to Atlanta, still alive, they returned having undone another bit of the system of segregation. Their sheer bravado was thrown in the face of hoses, dogs, nightsticks, and jail sentences, the strength and audacity of their youth and their belief in each other almost the only weapons they had. In a letter home, volunteer Margaret Aley described meeting the SNCC staff at that summer orientation:

> I've never known people like them before; they are so full of heart and life. They are not afraid to show their emotions, they cry when they are sad; they laugh and dance when they are happy. And they sing; they sing from their hearts and in their songs they tell of life, struggle, sadness, and beauty. They have a freeness of spirit that I've rarely seen. But I think that's because they don't worry about maintaining the status quo. When we arrived here Saturday, I had a feeling that I didn't belong. . . . [Now] somehow I feel like I've found something I've been looking for for a long time. I feel like I've finally come home. I now have no doubt that I belong here.[3]

Bob had encountered the SNCC staff on a visit to Atlanta earlier in the spring. As he stood around the SNCC office in the middle of the night, a truck screeched to a halt outside. The beautiful woman who had driven it through the night came striding into the room. She looked him over. "You coming down this summer?" she asked. "We need you." If ever a young man was lost in a heartbeat, it was Bob. Dazzled equally by her courage and her looks, wanting to belong in the room as she did, to drive a truck with that ferocity and nonchalance, he committed himself to join them—her?—for the summer.

To answer the hoses with his body.

We think of the supreme sacrifice as that which men make in time of war. As in war, the civil rights movement asked young people to risk their lives. Some did die, some went mad. Most survived, many thrived. Their charm and strength were essential to breaking up segregation. They arrived young, they left tested. To die, under such circumstances, was not the point: the point was that they were ready to die, if things turned out that way. After the disappearance of Chaney, Goodman, and Schwerner, Stuart Rawlings wrote in his journal,

> What are my personal chances? There are 200 COFO volunteers who have been working in the state a week, and three of them have already been killed. I shall be working in Forrest County, which is reputedly less violent than Neshoba County. But I shall be working on voter registration, which is more dangerous than work in Freedom Schools or Community Centers. There are other factors which must be considered, too—age, sex, experience and common sense. All considered, I think my chances of being killed are 2%, or one in fifty.[4]

One did not go alone, however. Perhaps the greatest import of the Freedom Summer project was that it bonded young people together so that they might face the great dangers that lay ahead. Rawlings wrote on June 25,

> It happened today. . . . We were watching the CBS TV show —about 100 of us. . . . Walter Cronkite told how the whole country was watching Mississippi. And then the television was singing our freedom song, "We shall overcome, we shall overcome. . . ." So we all joined hands and sang with the television. We sang with our hearts—"justice shall be done . . . we shall vote together . . . we shall live in freedom . . ." and then someone said, "Everybody hum softly," so we hummed, and a Negro by my side spoke . . . "You know what we're all doing. . . . We're moving the world. We're all here to bring all the people of Mississippi, all the peoples of this country, all the peoples of the world . . . together . . . we're bringing a new revolution of love, so let's sing out together once again now, everybody hand in

hand. . . ." "Deep in my heart, I do believe. Oh . . . we shall overcome some day." Stunned, I walked alone out into the night.
Life was beautiful. It was perfect. These people were me, and I
was them. Absolutely nothing came between us, as our hearts
felt the call to work toward a better world. . . . I felt that I could
and would devote my life to this kind of revolution. Alleluia.[5]

Nor were the volunteers alone when they arrived in Mississippi.
Bob describes a scene in a church. "The Klan was outside — they were
always outside. We sang. The preachers used to say that the singing
kept the devil away. Everybody knew everybody. It wasn't like they
were strangers in those small towns in Mississippi. To sing a freedom song was to make a declaration." A lot of those churches are
small, isolated buildings that were the soul of small, rural communities. They were (and remain) vulnerable to fires and bombs. Because
the churches were the meeting places, it was logical to try to destroy
them. To go to the churches, to sing in the churches, was to form
bonds between the volunteers, who were outsiders, and the people of
Mississippi, insiders to its disaster. Through those new connections,
all the people might welcome liberation.

Each new day, for Bob and the other volunteers, was a day of
learning. The elders of the movement, people like Ella Baker, who
had been around organizing in the South for years, guided the youthful organizers, offering advice and counsel. Not that it was always
taken: SNCC was running on youthful arrogance as much as anything.
The guidance, however, filtered down. There were ways to do things.
Ways to enter a town and win support from the local people. Ways
to run a Freedom Day, when people tried to register to vote. Ways to
drive a dark highway at night. Ways to avoid useless fights. Ways to
manage jail-time. Ways to say to people without education, "Fifty-
six percent of the people in the state are black, but only 2 percent of
the voters are black." All these things were taught, one by one.

Bob arrived, then, wanting to be one of this gang of cowboys.
He, too, has charm and charisma. Bob can preach, he can persuade,
he can convince. In the towns of Mississippi, he was a Native's Son
returned. His grandfather had practiced medicine in Yazoo City
for many years. His father had been born in Mississippi. The local

people took pride in seeing a young man who was doing well. They longed for education for themselves and their children, and Bob fit their dream of that future. To some extent, he was a wonder, a doctor's kid from the North, who was smooth and talked like white people. "I remember one day I was writing down the names for voter registration, and they were amazed that I could write fast. Many of them when they had to sign a paper could only make their mark. They gathered around and gave me pieces of paper. 'Hey, do that again,' they told me, marveling at how fast I could write. I was everybody's kid. I was Robin Hood, come home from the Crusades to overthrow the Sheriff of Nottingham."

He chuckles, remembering the two young men who worked with him, both white. They were terrified, as he was, and just wanted to survive. All three quickly figured out that Bob had the best ideas. He became the leader of the team. But they also figured out that the locals were entranced by the sight of a black man ordering two white men around. Somebody would come up to one of the white team members and ask a question. They would answer, "Oh, gee, I don't know, Bob's in charge." "He is?" would be the stunned response. It made for good theater. The three of them played it for all it was worth.

Bob was immersed in learning. Having grown up in Newark, he was somewhat prepared for the poverty he saw all around. People lived under terrible conditions in the poorest state in the nation. Houses lacked indoor plumbing, often they were little better than shacks. Yet people shared what they had with the volunteers.

He was shocked, as were other volunteers, by the intensity of the racism that permeated that world. As a youngster, he had gone to Mississippi to visit his grandfather shortly after the murder of Emmett Till. Helen Fullilove had impressed on her son the need to avoid offending white people. "This is not home," she warned, over and over. Bob arrived in 1964 with the image of Emmett Till burned in his brain. But there was more to racism in Mississippi than that. Blacks and whites had worked out odd compromises. Conditions were not uniform across the state: standards differed sharply from the Gulf area, which was the most liberal, to the more rural parts of the state.

But the violence of racism was ever present. "I was a middle-class doctor's kid who's never seen this stuff before. I arrived late, without status, and I had to learn how to survive." Bob laughs as he describes hearing a gunshot one night. Back at the SNCC office, he said, "Somebody shot at me." Ivanhoe Donaldson, one of the leading young men in the organization, and an important teacher for Bob, considered that idea.

"Somebody actually took a gun, pointed it at you, and tried to shoot you?"

"Well, not exactly."

"You mean they might have shot it in the air?"

"Well, I guess." As he tells this part of the story, he hunches his shoulders in imitation of the contrition of a young man being schooled by his elders.

"Fulli, did you ever hear of anybody being killed by a gun that was shot in the air?"

More contrition. "I guess not."

Later, the teasing would begin. The other young men would point their fingers in the air. "Hey, Fulli, pow, pow," and laugh uproariously at his discomfort.

It was important to know what was danger and what was simply harassment. The more Bob understood the threat, the better able he was to manage the fear.

There were many lessons. There were some victories. Bob discovered he could organize, that he had good ideas and people followed his suggestions. He learned that he had an intuitive sense for matching a person with a task to get the best result. He could easily assemble a team. If he never paid attention to details, that was rarely a problem because he always had a team member who did. He understood the components of a movement, largely that things had to get moving. That, he could do. He organized a Freedom Day in DeSoto that impressed Ivanhoe. "Good work, Fulli," was all Ivanhoe said, but he meant it. Sixty people showed up to register to vote. If the Reign of Terror was challenged by anything that summer, it was that people went public with their desire for equality. Sixteen thousand black people showed up at courthouses all around the state, trying to register. Few succeeded that summer, but they laid the groundwork for change. It was only by the public demonstration of injustice that the whole of the nation could understand what was going in Mississippi.

Not all was easy, though. Bob made some terrible errors. Woody Berry, a fellow student from Colgate, had worked hard to convince a local preacher to let them use his church for a meeting. Bob remembers getting into an argument over theology. "I was just showing off, but it gave the preacher an excuse to say, 'If you so smart, why don't you find some place else to meet?' It cost the team two weeks of work, and it was hard for them to forgive."

More difficult for everyone — men and women, white and black — was the ethos of risk-taking that suffused Freedom Summer, characterized by macho initiation rites that raised the blooded over the unblooded. Bob was timid. "I wanted to be there, but I didn't want to die." He drew a line on risk-taking and held it. This cost him in a setting that gave status points for gunshot wounds and jail-time. Oddly, as an adult, he is comforted by his ability then to say "no." Resisting peer pressure gave him a sense of himself that he came to treasure. "The most courageous thing I did as a young man was not to reject being middle class. People tried to get on me about being a doctor's kid. I said, 'Yeah, I'm a doctor's kid. And you know what, the people of Mississippi respect that!'" In fact, his own conservative choices were much closer to those made daily by the people of Mississippi than were those of the radical leaders of SNCC who had come to Mississippi from places far away.

It was a summer of terror and joy. It was erotic. It was transformative. The Movement, in those days, had a rhetoric and a practice that could be life-consuming. It was easy, in the urgency of the era, when lives were truly on the line, to imagine that The Movement was all there was. The Movement provided activity and friends, places to be, and things to think about. One could be immersed in it. As the summer came to an end, some, including Bob, wanted to stay. Bob's parents held him back from staying. His dad said, "No, you're not. You're going back to school."

With mixed feelings, Bob headed back to Colgate University and a winter of dreaming. This was a difficult time for many. The end of August 1964 was a sharply etched point in the lives of the Freedom

Summer volunteers. They had been on a rescue mission. They had been to a disaster site, a place where democracy had been shanghaied by racism. They had challenged centuries' old traditions. They had made a difference. More than that had happened, though. They had lived in a new way. Young adults had lived together without older adults around to comment on their actions. They were free to be friends and lovers as they chose. They had tasted sexual and social liberation. Were they to go back to something less important, less free, less joyous, less honest?

Bob returned to Colgate a changed person. "It would have been much better if someone I knew had gone. It would have set some limits on my self-righteousness, then. It would have provided perspective. As it was, I was insufferable. I had been slightly above average in Mississippi. But I had gone to Mississippi. My friends had been too afraid." Bob had gone a boy, come back a man. He was transformed by the opportunity to test his limits, by the chance to be immersed in change, by the occasion to make a difference. Like many others returning from the South, he was someone different. Part of it was a new black identity, a radical consciousness born on those truck rides through the night. Part of it was that he had gone in search of the coveted Grail.

Bob stayed close to SNCC, returning the next summer and joining its staff after college. He was coming to the end of his time with SNCC when I first met him. By then I was seventeen and had finished my first year of college. He was twenty-four and newly married to his first wife. He was definitely one of the SNCC folk, defined as they all were by having absorbed both the South and the swagger of those Freedom Summers. I didn't like the SNCC men very much. They lorded their age and their experience over me like I was a peon. They didn't want to listen to me, and I wanted to be heard. Therefore, I had little use for them.

But even in such a crowd, Bob's warmth was a discernible, memorable force. He noticed me not at all. He didn't notice me the second time we met either, though, again, I was thoroughly energized by his presence.

The third time we met was in 1982, just as I was finishing my residency in psychiatry and ending my first marriage. When I learned that he would be speaking at a local conference, I felt a frisson throughout my body. I wasn't going to take any chances that he would ignore me again. If it took heat and light to get noticed, I was going to crank up the generator. I wore a black dress. It was a drizzly day in late spring, and I worried that my dress would get soggy and my hair frizzy. I sought out Milton Brown, the man I was then dating, organizer of the conference and friend of Bob. He introduced us. "So, Mindy, this is Bob Fullilove. I know you've been wanting to meet him." I turned to Bob and smiled.

I had been practicing this smile. It was meant to convey electricity, dazzle, excitement. He was supposed to conclude, on the basis of that smile, that he *must* get to know me, *must* pay attention to me. It would transfix, titillate, entangle. I did all this with Milton watching the whole thing, but I didn't notice. I was caught up in history: my time had come. That I was bent on seduction I managed to hide from my conscious mind. Milton describes as "stunning" the moment my smile caught Bob: Milton was entirely clear what I was doing, even if I was not.

Bob was thoroughly engaged. He got the impression that I was coming on to him—which was actually more than I had admitted to myself—and he didn't hesitate to respond. What a mess. That took a few months—and more than a little help from Milton, bless his heart—to sort out.

That morning, however, Bob and I talked, and I immediately felt that I had met my best friend. All that warmth and power were as real as I had imagined, and I was desperately in love. Within minutes of meeting him, I had poured out my troubles. I told him that I was about to start a job directing a day hospital, and I was worried about succeeding. He scoffed at the idea that I might fail. This was hardly a challenge, he seemed to say. I didn't realize then how he marked his scale. No one was likely to shoot at me (or even over my head). My life was safe, even if my pride was on the line: I simply had to make friends in order to succeed.

Bob knew how to make friends. From an early age he understood his parents had in mind for him to be an ambassador of sorts. Helen and Robert Fullilove had been limited by segregation. Robert had done a fellowship at Harvard University, and he was one of a handful of black physicians of his era to have had such an opportunity. But there was no career path outside the black community that he could pursue. Helen ran every organization that came within her purview, but she too was restricted always and everywhere by the color bar. They had fought hard to take down those restrictions. "Someone," they said to their son, "has got to take advantage of these opportunities that we've worked so hard to create."

It was not hard for him to enter the white world. In 1957, he and two other boys were the first blacks to enter Pingry, a select private school in Elizabeth, New Jersey. On the first day of school, an eighth-grade boy came up to Bob, shook his hand, put his arm around his shoulder, and introduced him to his friends. Once in the circle, Bob began to converse. It was easy. After the streets of Newark, the halls of Pingry, with their rules and dignity, would pose no challenge. The fastest boy in his grade challenged him to a race later that first day. In the way of boys, Bob easily beat him and the two became friends. Bob came home from his first day of school realizing that he had skills. He was poised, he had charm, and he was *fast*. Pingry prepared Bob for SNCC and the Freedom Summer.

But let's return to King Arthur's point about the knights of the Round Table: Arthur predicted that few of those who left on the search for the Grail would ever return. Percivale, for example, entered a monastery and took holy vows. Recognizing that he was a knight from Arthur's court, a monk asked what had happened to make Percivale forsake the Round Table. The Knight answers that it was

But the sweet vision of the Holy Grail
Drove me from all vainglories, rivalries,
And earthly heats that spring and sparkle out
Among us in the jousts, while women watch
Who wins, who falls, and waste the spiritual strength
Within us, better offer'd up to Heaven.[6]

For Percivale the power of the Grail was such that, having seen it, he had to live in a new way. It was a turning point. The life of a knight no longer suited. In order to satisfy his spirit, Percivale immersed himself in the life of a monastery.

The vision offered by the Freedom Summer—a vision of equality and dignity for all people—likewise transformed Bob, from a happy schoolboy into a man of the spirit. Where would he go next? The line from a World War I song—"How you gonna keep 'em down on the farm after they've seen Paris?"—is more about Verdun and the other great battles of the war than it is about furlough in a European capital. A boy goes to war. If he returns, he comes back a man. Where does he now fit, and how?

Bob, ambassador to the world, returned from the South with a newfound manliness. He could not return to his parents' home as the child they had sent away. Even more dramatically, the home of his childhood was destroyed—another highway taking another family's house—shortly after he returned. The cumulative toll of these events was a sense of rootlessness, that he could go anywhere and do anything, but that place itself had no meaning. He embarked on a journey: attending Union Theological Seminary to avoid the draft; heading off with Woody Berry to run a program for underprivileged youth in Syracuse, where he also got a Master's degree in instructional technology; returning to New York for doctoral study at Teachers' College; spending a few years in Trenton with the State Department of Education; heading to Washington DC to work for the Fund for the Improvement of Postsecondary Education (FIPSE), a small but glitzy part of the U.S. Department of Education that gave him room to fund ideas he liked. In 1983 he convinced me to join him in his trek. We moved to Berkeley, where we married and set up our first home.

It added up to twenty-nine moves in twenty years, and in all those moves, he lost his memories. Memory depends on sights and sounds; it must be interrogated and stirred. Otherwise, the stored information falls, inert, to the bottom of whatever holds information in the brain. It is essentially lost. Bob often contrasts himself with his friend Warren Barksdale, a classmate at Teachers' College who is immersed in the places and the networks of his early life, and—there-fore, perhaps—has ready access to the memories of his youth.

Bob might have gone on drifting, rootless and unconcerned. As fate would have it, Bob, Molly, my youngest child who was then nine, and I went to Stockholm for the AIDS conference in 1988. After the con-ference, we traveled in Europe, first to Copenhagen, then Cologne, and then Paris. We had an awful time in Cologne. We arrived early in the morning, after sleeping on the train. It was unexpectedly cold and rainy. Because it was Monday, the tourist attractions were closed. We wandered from coffee shop to coffee shop, trying to amuse our-selves. I invented a game called the Mystery of Cologne. It was a treasure hunt, and I promised that, when all the treasures had been collected, we would understand the Mystery of Cologne. At the end of our search, I offered a solution to the puzzle:

1. Never go to Cologne.
2. Never especially go to Cologne on Monday.
3. Don't go anywhere on Monday.
4. Don't go anywhere early in the morning.
5. If you go early, leave early.
6. If you have to do any of the above, do it with people you love![7]

"You're so corny," Bob and Molly groaned. By then, it was 9 P.M., and there was nothing left to do but sit bleary-eyed in the station, feeling the seconds eke by as we waited for our train to Paris.

The train, when it came, was cozy and delightful. The sleeper car had two berths, one above the other. Each berth had crisp, sweet-smelling sheets and warm blankets. A man came by and offered cof-fee from a little cart. We slept deeply as the train rumbled through the night. We got off at 7 A.M. and made our way through the sta-tion to the street. It was very quiet, and there wasn't a lot of traffic. We stood there, facing a typical Parisian street: low, white buildings etched against a blue sky and at each window a box of red geraniums.

We crossed the street to a brasserie opposite the station. We walked in, unsure of our welcome, and sat down. The waiter came over with a benevolent look on his face and said, "Bonjour" in a deep throaty voice, heavy with cigarettes and wine. "Qu'est-ce que vous voulez?" Bob managed to explain that we wanted café-au-lait and croissants. "Le petit déjeuner complet?" he asked. Yes, that. There has never been a croissant more flaky, coffee more delicious, or strawberry jam sweeter than what we ate that morning.

For Bob, it was a moment of homecoming. If he had been rootless, he was not rootless anymore. If he had eschewed memories, he did no longer. To speak French became The Way, and he literally entered a new realm of being; he became interior to it. Although he knew a good deal of French from his high school and college studies, upon our return to the States he dedicated himself to the task of mastering the language. He began to spend five hours a day learning to speak French. He listened to tapes and watched TV, scribbled in grammar books, and mumbled to himself.

Watching Bob's immersion in his French life was profoundly disturbing to me. I watched him enter it, and I felt as if he were leaving me. Since 1986 we had been deeply involved in AIDS research and were, by 1988, coleaders of a small research group. We had been in the habit of chatting about work as we drove across the Bay Bridge from our home in Berkeley to our office in San Francisco. Though we still drove to work together, he would no longer talk to me because he was listening to French tapes. When we visited Paris in April 1989, all he thought about was his vocabulary. He would sit in French restaurants, eavesdropping on other people's conversations and chuckling to indicate that he *understood French.* He would stop French-accented people and tell them he had learned French at the university.

One summer, he virtually imported a young French woman into his office, ostensibly so he could practice speaking French. They talked for hours every day. He was shocked that I considered this an affront; I was stunned that he didn't understand how unsettling it was for me to have my husband conversing for hours a day with an all-too-eager young blonde. I was not comforted that she was a bottle blonde.

The way that he created time for his studies was by a drastic

alteration in his role in the research group we co-led, ceding responsibility for grants and projects to me. Since I was in most respects a
very junior partner, the enterprise floundered for a long time before
I found a body of work I could manage independently.

I was completely mystified by this whole situation. What had happened to my husband? What had happened to my marriage? Bob's
love of French was not obvious, or superficial, or utilitarian. He
swore that it in no way diminished his love of me or devotion to our
family, but that didn't help me understand what it *was.*

"What does it all mean?" became a frequent topic of conversation,
but in many ways Bob's life transformation had no simple "meaning."
Rather, he entered a new way of life that strikes me as what Percivale did after he entered the monastery. Things began to make sense
only when I started to ask, "What is a monastic way of life?"

A central feature of that lifestyle—and here I am greatly aided
by the writing of Kathleen Norris, who has shared monastic life as
a Benedictine oblate—is the ordering of life around spiritual practice. As Norris describes it, the monks' lives are structured around
the reading of Scripture and the celebration of holy services at specific intervals throughout the day. Every monastery, I gather, has
a posted schedule of these activities. For example, the Saint John's
Abbey Liturgy Schedule is

7 A.M.	Morning Prayer
NOON	Noon Prayer
5 P.M.	Eucharist
7 P.M.	Vespers
11:30 A.M.	Saturday Eucharist
10:30 A.M.	Sunday Eucharist[8]

Spiritual practice is, quite literally and like all practice, the constant repetition of the required works. Again, as is the case with
practice, it leads to spiritual development, it leads toward perfection.

I ask Bob to write out his French schedule for me. He is a little
puzzled by my request. "It's not the same every day," he replies. Suddenly—after all these years—I know that I am on firm ground, and

I insist that there is a "French schedule" to his day. Suddenly he brightens and sets to work. It takes a few minutes for him to outline the themes and variations that structure his life:

Bob's List of French Self-Teaching Activities

Overall organizing theme

At least two hours per day in either listening to, reading, or speaking French (and yes, I do keep a tally! I won't go to bed if I haven't put in the time!!)—prior to 1993, this was four hours per day. Number of days I spent every free moment doing something French? I lost count! Number of times since 1988 I have taken a day off (that is, done no French whatsoever): *none.*

Typical weekday at home

a. one hour of RFI in the A.M.—on a day when I am not due at the office, I do the whole broadcast (6:30 to 9:00)

b. three articles per day in either *L'Express* or *Journal français d'amerique*

c. If I get home before Mindy, one lesson of *French in Action* (30 minutes) on TV

Typical weekend day at home

a. all of RFI (always, especially Saturday, 6:30–10 A.M.)

b. one French-in-Action lesson

c. one "grammar exercise" (go through a difficult article or part of a French book with a French [as opposed to a French/English] dictionary and the *500 French Verbs* book [for practice with the more exotic verb forms]) Now that I have the *Petit Robert,* this exercise can be done entirely with that new toy!

d. minimum of one-half hour of reading anything French (preferably something with dialogue to see the conversational forms)

e. taking notes of some aspect of all of the above!

Typical travel period

a. minimum two Champs Elysées tapes (plus transcription) one tape in the morning before breakfast; the other at night (one side of each tape per session)

b. minimum one *L'Express* and one *Journal Français*

c. "troll" for French speakers (spend time in a public place with a visible French publication to attract the attention of someone who will say the magic words "Vous parlez . . . ?") hit/success rate? approximately 5%

Miscellaneous

Any "significant" time spent speaking French to someone, particularly on the phone, "counts" as one element in any of the lists above. If I feel I've screwed up (stumbled over a verb for example), I must go resolve any question that may linger (most typical example? reviewing the choice of the verb and/or checking the gender of a word [m/f])

Most frequently used trick to make sure I've maintained the purity of my resolve: have a conversation with myself. This is usually an exercise during which I tell a story to an imaginary French listener. If I stumble over a word/verb form (whatever!), I make a note and look up the troublemaker at some later time when I have a dictionary, thesaurus, etc.

The three pilars of this process: Champs Elysées, *French in Action* (particularly the workbooks), RFI.

Reinforcement (à la B. F. Skinner): have no conversation with a French speaker that does not include a compliment for my French!

Core Fundamental Concept: As I once remarked to a French speaker who asked "mais vous êtes français, vous, n'est-ce pas?" after a few minutes of conversation, "non, disons, plutôt, que j'ai l'esprit français."

He often tries to describe to me what it is like on the interior of his life. While in France, a friend recommended the CD-ROM version of *Le Petit Robert,* a popular French dictionary. With this dictionary, Bob can follow the trail of a word, looking up its meaning and its use, distinguishing it from close synonyms, exploring antonyms, and reading excerpts of text in which the word is used. He takes me to the computer and walks me through this search. His eyes are shining with the joy of this new toy. He is content.

I give him Alice Kaplan's *French Lessons* to read and he is profoundly moved.[9] She describes her antennae for French conversation and he feels he has found a peer. He reads passages to me, to share his admiration with this woman who actually worked with Pierre Capretz, the inventor of *French in Action* and Bob's foremost hero of French teaching.

In the meantime, I realize that, in addition to a remarkable fluency that startles French people, the endless effort has paid off in a profound understanding of human language. For example, Bob has oriented himself to hear the many layers of meaning a word carries. A television producer proposes to say that people have a physical dependence on food. Bob stops her. "What is the connotation of 'physical dependence'?" He points out that the negative emotional reaction to the phrase will interfere with the message the producer wishes to convey. Because people are linked to each other by words, his close attention to their words and movements reveals to him the depths of the human spirit.

This leads me to the next, and most truly useful, question. I am convinced that Bob's immersion in French is the equivalent of Percivale's immersion in a monastic life. Now I must try to understand: "How is it that learning French is a spiritual discipline?" I find the answer through Kathleen Norris. She described a talk she gave to a group of Trappist monks.

> I told the monks that I had come to see both writing and monasticism as vocations that require periods of apprenticeship and formation. Prodigies are common in mathematics, but extremely rare in literature, and I added, 'As far as I know, there are no prodigies in monastic life.' The monks nodded, obviously amused. . . . Related to this, I said, was recognizing the dynamic nature of both disciplines; they are not so much subjects to be mastered as ways of life that require continual conversion. . . . The spiritual dimension of this process is humility, not a quality often associated with writers, but lurking

there, in our nagging sense of the need to revise, to weed out the lies you've told yourself and get real.[10]

These sentences describe, as well as anything I've seen or read, the life that Bob has led since that day in Paris. His path is, without question, a spiritual path in which learning French provides the liturgy. It is a life of continual conversion, of constant humility. Through the window of this discipline, he has come to understand the soul.

Though I have gained, with time and reflection, a better understanding of Bob's calling, it remains outside my experience. When I was fourteen, Bob was not. Though we lived a few miles apart, we lived in spheres defined by age and opportunity. I was too young to go to Mississippi; my life was defined by other challenges. Bob and I orbit closely, intimately, but on separate planes. We saw that Paris day with different eyes. Like Percivale, Bob had followed the Grail. He entered the City of Light looking for a spiritual center. I meditate often on Arthur's dark prophesy: "Go, since your vows are sacred, being made. . . . Many of you, yea most, return no more." I think there is no going back from the call of the Grail, only a going forward. The profound and careful practice of spiritual discipline is a possible next step.

FOUNDLINGS

In my foster houses
I had 15 sisters and no brothers
I was four months
I had nine sisters and one brother
I was nine months
I had three sisters and four brothers
at age two and a half
Now I'm Kenny Kaufman age four
Bye everybody
I'm going home

Kenny Kaufman
"Foster Home," 1979

I have mothered four children, three grievously injured before I met them, the fourth hurt in the course of family dissension. It is no small thing for children to get on with their lives after parents have failed them. My teacher during psychiatric residency, Estelle Schecter, once said that you could follow childhood injury like a red thread coursing through the life path. This thread of pain was an intrinsic part of being. She taught that healing lay in reconfiguring the injury, making something of the scar tissue, if you will. She delighted in sending me little drawings of new ways to see my own world as a safer, more solid place.

Healing my children, to the extent I was able, required of me that I hold the center. It required of them, I learned in the course of events, that they take responsibility for their own power.

I was not a naturally gifted mother. I got into parenting to keep my first marriage together and with little idea of what would be required of me. The day before I became a parent, my basic plan was not to make the mistakes my parents had made. The day after I became a parent I just wanted to know how they had kept at it for twenty-four years. The idea that one ought to hold the center came to me gradually. Night after night I insisted that the family turn off the television to gather for dinner and talk. "Aw, Ma, we're not like you, we don't want to talk. We just want to eat," they'd say. "Just tell me about your day," I would say. I nearly gave in at one point, but then I thought, "No, it is right for a family to get together and talk." So I continued to insist, and they continued to fuss.

It's easier to hold the center if there are shared values to define that middle ground. From the beginning, that was not what the family was. My then-husband, Mike, was a genuinely nice guy, tender-hearted, patient, and somewhat timid. He was content to slide through life, avoiding the world of challenge. I was, in my early twenties, socially phobic but eager to meet the world and conquer it. He was homebound, I was not: this was to be a fundamental tension in figuring out how to share parenting.

In 1975, Mike and I adopted Kenny, a rambunctious four-year-old with a strong will and a decided sense of humor. Kenny, by a failure of the system, had been kept in foster care for four years after he had been freed by his birth mother. He had grown to love his foster parents and they him. He loved their suburban house and their lifestyle. They had a big pool in the backyard. Kenny could swim in the back and ride his bigwheels in the front. There were always kids to play with and cake to eat. He was a truly happy little guy. As an adult, his life ambitions are largely to re-create the life that he had as a four-year-old in foster care. The shock of being "took-en away," as he used to say, was overwhelming. In the way of children, he hadn't known that he didn't belong. His grief was deep. But worse, he moved from his suburban idyll to a small apartment in a hostile city. He had no skills for city life. He didn't fit in. He was dreadfully lonely. If ever a child felt misused by the world, it was Ken.

Even in the midst of transplantation shock, Ken had a point of view that was distinctly his own. He was ferociously stubborn and believed in his own ideas. Four-year-olds, like Ken, can reason, but they are not yet able to test their conclusions. Kenny tenaciously held on to some very kooky ideas; formed at four in the midst of upheaval, they became the foundation of his style. He had a remarkable streak of independence, combined with a talent for managing crisis. The second day after he came to live with us, he and I became separated. I was walking into a store slightly ahead of him. I looked back and he was gone. I was panicked. I couldn't imagine what I was going to tell the adoption agency: "I'm so sorry, he was quite a little guy, but I lost him at the supermarket"? My plans for parenthood were melting. But not so. Kenny had simply found someone to take him home and was there waiting for me. Kenny, through all his troubles, didn't look for advice: he wanted to manage on his own.

A fourth, and truly unique, view of the world, was added by Dina Tracy Shepard, who joined our family in 1977. Dina was, even at four, a human powerhouse. She walked up to Kenny, the first time she met him, and said, "Hi, Ugly." Having taken the offensive—and I do mean offensive—she never let up. She says of herself then, "I was a tornado. I wanted everything. Nobody else could have anything because I needed it. I needed all the attention, but when I got it, I didn't know what to do with it." In fact, the attention was so often negative that she became increasingly aggrieved rather than satisfied. Her lust for the world consumed us all. "Did the adoption agency tell you what you were getting into?" she asks me. As well she might. Who knew, then, what it really meant to raise children who had been exposed to drugs while in the womb, hospitalized for long periods of time during infancy, physically abused while in foster care, and then given up for adoption? As the evidence has accumulated—from adoptions of drug-exposed babies, as well as overseas adoptions of neglected children—it has become clear what a formidable challenge this is. Some families have been so beleaguered that they have given the children back, unable to face the financial and emotional costs abused children can extract from their would-be rescuers. On nothing were Mike and I so divided as on the management of our little whirlwind. He was all tenderness and concern, I was all limits and discipline, each of us too polar to be much good.

Molly came in 1979, a sweet and kind baby, who didn't ask for much and gave great joy to all who met her. This was the kind of sister Kenny had wanted, and he took to her with gusto. Dina was deeply threatened because the baby, without doing anything, got everything Dina wanted but didn't know how to achieve.

I learned, as I emerged from the haze of pregnancy, that, three children later, I still didn't want that marriage. In 1981, Mike and I agreed to divorce.

A year later, I met Bob at the fateful third meeting, and a new world began for me. We began to put together a new family that included, in addition to my three children, his son, Bobby. Bobby was another wounded soul. Everyone who ever met her describes Bobby's mother as quite mad. A beautiful woman, wonderfully smart, a great dancer, but unable to manage human relationships. She was distant and cold. I imagine that she was never emotionally available for Bobby. She abandoned the scene completely when he was seven. After that he lived with Bob, which meant that he was uprooted and moved all over the East Coast by his vagabond dad. Bobby, like Dina, was desperate for love and attention. He was less of a tornado, however, and confined his grabs for attention to intermittent thefts and occasional episodes of running away. At five, he stole fifty dollars from his grandmother, the first of many announcements that he couldn't tolerate the loneliness. Bob, though a dutiful father, was no help in that department. If Bobby was fed and housed, Bob felt he had done his part: he was not the kind of guy for bedtime stories and games of catch.

Christmas 1982 was our first big holiday together. I was broke, but Bob arrived with his paycheck to fill the gap. My mother, Bob, and I went to the mall on Christmas Eve and shopped to our hearts' content. It was blissful to buy stuff for our kids. The tree was grand and looked beautiful with all the presents underneath. Christmas was unseasonably warm — it reached sixty-three degrees by midday. Bob, our boys, and the young men in the neighborhood played touch football in the big driveway of my house. I made pancakes and bacon, and we ate heartily. Christmas dinner was a real feast. All of us reveled in the day. It was more like a wartime truce than a real peace, however, since bitter custody battles lay ahead. Mike couldn't bear the idea that his kids would become family with Bob. Dina, fighting on his side, went on the attack. By summer, Bob and I had settled in California with the two boys, while Dina and Molly stayed in New Jersey with Mike.

Blended families have two strikes against them on the shared values front. First, individuals come to the family from different backgrounds. Their ideas are likely to clash. Second—and the most severe problem for us—the loss of the first family may so undermine faith that individuals come to the second family unwilling to believe in it. Like Tinkerbell, a family has a claim to life only if its members believe. My four children have little enough reason to be that trusting.

I have no doubt, based on my observations of Bobby, Kenny, Dina, and Molly, that children are liberally and genetically endowed with an unchanging self. The part that parents can play in bringing up baby is to be gentle and consistent. Parents who fail in those tasks undermine the child's trust. The untrusting child grows to maturity seeing authority as the enemy rather than as an ally. Abandoned children, certainly my three adopted children—and even Molly to some extent—view words that come from the mouths of adults as "Lies, damned lies, and statistics!" There are a number of ways that the children demonstrated their distrust of authority. First, they never asked for advice. They kept as much of their lives away from us as they could. Second, they felt entitled to break rules. Rules, after all, were made by the authorities that they didn't trust; to save themselves, they had the right to do as they saw fit. Third, they didn't accept the need to share with others. They were convinced that they could—and should—take what they needed.

The children, then, were disposed to pull against the center. It was my job to be the counterweight. It became Bob's job to make sure I wasn't *too* weighty. I would tell him, "Bob, you have to support me in [whatever]." "OK," he would say. Then he would tell the kids, "Your mother made me swear that I'd support her in [whatever], so I can't help you in this." I had been raised on the philosophy of Frantz Fanon, the famous black psychiatrist from Martinique who argued that violence was transforming for the colonized soul. As Martin Luther King Jr. pointed out in arguing for nonviolence, any admission of violence was a slippery slope. If violence is endorsed in one situation, is it not all right in others? Bob's checks on me, and mine on him, were an important brake on our tendency to depend on harsh physical discipline and angry shouting to get the family moving in the right direction.

One of my children once complained that he (or she, I forget who posed this complaint) thought that I was experimenting on them. There is a certain truth to that statement. I was neither so well prepared for parenting as I thought I would be nor so supported by my children that it didn't matter. They were determined to test me on every issue. If spanking and shouting didn't work—and believe me, they didn't—what was I to do? To even the odds a little, I read every book I could find and pumped every child psychiatrist and family therapist I met.

The children chuckled at much of it, liked some of it, were unaffected by lots of it. When Kenny first came to live with us, he cried every night. My therapist urged me to sympathize with his loss. At the time, I was so excited to be a new mother that sympathizing with his loss was quite a foreign idea. I wanted him to be as happy as I was. Instead, we commiserated nightly about the horrors of losing the only home he had ever known. Little did I understand then how much the move from a comfortable suburban home to a city apartment had displaced him from a lifestyle he loved to one he hated. Even less did I get the full weight of how a four-year-old would take the strange turn of events in which his wonderful foster parents had let some yokels take him away from the swimming pool *where he really belonged.*

When Dina started setting fires in the yard, my teacher, Estelle, advised a behavioral reinforcement schedule. Every night after dinner, Dina lit matches. This was done with careful attention to ritual. Opening the book of matches, taking out a match, closing the book of matches, lighting the match, and dousing it in a bowl of water. We did a book a night for a week, and that was the end of fire setting. Of course, Dina, the human tornado, was on to the next act of insurrection, and I was left to search for the next solution.

Bobby broke my heart because he was an underachiever. He was brilliant in all things scholastic. He had perfect spelling and grammar, an enviable sense of storytelling, and no wish to go to school. For the first month of school in California he cut his seventh-period biology class. We solved that with sheets initialed by each teacher and turned in at the end of the day. Ever-resourceful Bobby just went to class and tuned out.

I thought I had reached the pinnacle of family management when we had a complex, multicolored chart on which we tracked chores, allowances, and activities. This chart was the subject of regular meetings, held on Sundays, after we had cleaned house and consumed pancakes. Ahh. They still managed to underachieve in school, taunt their siblings, and flaunt some kind of authority. Rarely mine: I was too loud, and I had the chart. But someone's. Teachers were particularly vulnerable to attack and suffered badly at the hands of my children. I had a stunning experience one day when I called to find out why my brilliant daughter Molly had not been accepted to Manhattan Friends, a prestigious private high school. "Our students have a lot of responsibility," a chilling voice said. "We just can't have students who fail to cooperate." It was the revenge of Molly's English teacher, who was Russian and thought American girls, especially Molly, were much too "bold." "How can you be so *bold?*" she would demand of them. I begged and pleaded with Molly to stop torturing her teachers. "They're stupid," was all she would say. "They were stupid," she says now. Even if they were, did that mean they had to be punished and that *she* had to do it? Maybe the teachers couldn't help being stupid. This line of reasoning got me nowhere.

Bob and I slowly learned that the most powerful tool we had was our ability to determine the settings in which our children passed their lives. When we first arrived in Berkeley, in the summer of 1983, Bob went to the high school to try to register Bobby. He learned that, because of the bureaucracy involved, it would be weeks into the school year before we could get this done. In the meantime, we began to hear horror stories from other black families. Although the school had a large proportion of black students, only a handful were on the college track. The rest were on the road to becoming thugs. This was not what we wanted or what we thought Bobby needed. We learned about Saint Mary's College High School, a Catholic college preparatory school for boys, that was largely nonwhite and sent 99 percent of its graduates for further education. Bobby, by the end of his first year there, had managed to attend some classes, had stopped "tuning out," and was making a name for himself in sports.

Kenny had enrolled in the local public schools and had strayed onto a negative path. He and his friends were constantly being suspended from school for misbehaving in class or for other misdeeds. In fact, Bob and I used to have a ritual that, if we called each other in the morning, we had to leave a message saying, "*Not* an emergency." Messages without that tag meant that one of the two boys was suspended from school or in some other kind of trouble. The school's policy of suspension was in the same ridiculous vein of using violence to control children. Getting sent away from school as undesirable did nothing to shore up Kenny's wish to study and learn. Repeatedly thrown out, he wasn't the sort of kid to fight to get back in. He became more and more entrenched in the role of outsider. Things were quickly going from bad to worse. It was obvious, by spring, that he would not be on the college track in the high school: he would be in the thug contingent, with little hope of being prepared for higher education.

I was frantic. I was no dyed-in-the-wool adherent to public education. I wanted my child to be able to get a college education. Everything that was going on was lessening his chances. His behavior and the school's behavior were both undermining his learning. We turned again to Saint Mary's. Kenny was really distressed. His friends at school called him a faggot because he would be going to a boys' school. He was pained and alienated. It took months for him to settle in. But gradually he looked around and realized that he was in the midst of a different but likeable group of boys. They were cool, but they studied. They played sports, and they dreamed about the future. They were planning to have big houses with swimming pools. Kenny could relate to this plan. He could work with this, albeit with suspicion, keeping the Christian Brothers who ran the school at arm's length. One day he came home from school in a particularly good mood. They had been on a retreat with a nearby girls' school, and they had spent the day in trust-building exercises. In a moment of expansiveness unusual for Ken, he told me about the different activities. "You know, they put a blindfold on you and someone leads you around. Or you lean back and they catch you. You have to trust. It was nice. I had a good time."

The more I saw what it meant to be in the "right" settings, the more I tried to understand the qualities that made a setting work. One of these is *positive,* Ken's word for settings that convey hope for the future and attachment to community. *Negative* settings, on his scale, are filled with alienation and despair. After leaving college he had a job installing computer equipment in schools. The wealthy schools he visited were uniformly clean and the teachers seemed concerned about their students. By contrast, the poor schools were filthy and the teachers were abusive toward students. "I've never seen a teacher in those schools take a kid aside and just talk to him. They just yell and scream." Ken moved to Atlanta, at age twenty-four, because he felt that it was a more positive place for a young black man like himself than the New York–New Jersey area in which he had grown up. "This is home," he says. "But Atlanta has more opportunity. I don't know—it's just more positive."

Another quality is *acceptance.* People need to feel they belong in the setting. Kids are especially happy if they are acknowledged. Dina and Bobby, in their panicky efforts for attention, were expressing an extreme version of all kids' need for affection. Molly loved third and fourth grades at Cleveland School in Englewood because she felt accepted there. She was the teacher's pet: she felt that school was made for her. During that happy period she undertook the Martin Luther King Jr. essay contest. She entered every year with the hope of winning, moving slowly up the ranks until she won the school contest and got honorable mention at the state level. She felt so welcome that it was not a problem for her to try to do her best.

A third quality is *fun.* Kids really like to play. They like to run and jump and do interesting things. For several summers, Molly went to a daycamp in Berkeley that she really liked. She remembers the things they used to do there. "We'd go out and pick blackberries and come back and make a blackberry pie. Or we'd go to the beach or the water slide. We had adventures. It was fun." Kenny, too, remembers Berkeley with fondness because he learned to play basketball there. There was room on the courts around town for a kid with more heart than talent. Kenny played and played, thousands and thousands of games, until even Bobby — the much more talented player — acknowledged that he had a sweet game.

If the settings in the outside world were important, so too, were the private retreats they created, away from the fears of abandonment and betrayal. Some of it went on in their rooms. Some of it had to do with going away from home, to other houses where they were not under the pressures of family. Some of it was emotional retreat. Going away — whatever that meant, whatever it took — was an important part of their actions toward us during the growing-up years. The first time my son Bobby looked me in the eye and told me his feelings, I thought I would die from joy. But he was twenty-eight and I was forty-five before we managed to accomplish that. Meanwhile, my kids often went outside of our space to feel in touch with themselves and their own ideas of life. At some point, each of them used that aloneness to think about themselves.

Kenny, battling us over school, had a dazzling insight into his life while walking down the street. He saw a bum and thought the man looked pathetic, cold, dirty, and disgusting, without shelter on a rainy day. Kenny realized, quite suddenly, that he didn't want to be pathetic when he was an adult. He was so shaken by this insight that he began to study. He brought his grades up to a B average, ensuring that he could get into a decent college.

The opposite of "going out" — letting us know we were on the right track — was rare, but ever so touching when it happened. Once, when Kenny was little, he and I watched *Old Yeller.* The end, which is so sorrowful, overwhelmed him. He leaned against me and let me hold him while he cried. He didn't say anything, then or later — he just let me hold him. We also used to go and sit on top of the Palisades and sing. Kenny loves to sing. He has a terrible voice, but that doesn't interfere with his pleasure in singing. And so we used to

loss. We cannot avoid loss: we can make, sometimes, something of it. We can find meaning in life even though it is not perfect.

Dina was, surprisingly enough, the first of the children to begin to explore the spiritual dimension of her life experience. In her very Dina way, she had started to go to church to meet a man. One day, as she was sitting in the service, she suddenly felt the presence of the Holy Spirit inside her. She felt saved and transformed by a sense of joy she had not known before. As she started to think of her life in relationship to God, she suddenly began to think about how she would use her power, whether for good or for evil. This was an extraordinary new dimension in one who as a child had deeply believed she was entitled to relieve her pain by taking from others. In God she found an authority in whom she might trust. This does not mean that the old Dina is gone. "My landlord came up and started bothering me. He thinks, just because I stay home with my children, that I'm some weak little thing. He doesn't know Dina. He started to yell at me, so I just had to get crazy back at him. I'm still Dina, even though I'm trying to be a Christian."

The new selves, trying to find positive settings, trying to be positive people, contain the injured children who had other strategies for managing life.

When I started to learn about the psychology of place, I asked friends and family to give me any books they thought might help. Molly said, "Here, read this. It's one of my favorite books and it's about place." It was a children's book called *The Boxcar Children.*[1] It tells the story of four children who, orphaned by the death of their parents, flee from a grandfather they fear. They try to make their own way in the world. They put together a comfortable life, living in the woods in an abandoned boxcar. Eventually, they meet their grandfather and learn to love him. He takes them to his mansion. Yet they miss their old life. He surprises them by installing the boxcar in the backyard so they can enjoy the things they loved there whenever they want.

This book sat on my desk for more than a year before I finally got it. The boxcar children fear authority. They construct an alternate world. As their trust in authority grows, they are willing to relinquish control, but they yearn for the world they had created for themselves. It is incorporated into the grandfather's house as a kind of retreat. They can come and go, as they please. It is the motion between worlds that struck such a profound chord. This was what I had been watching all those years. Subtle and obvious moves across space. Come close, pull away, near and far. Children incessantly testing the strength of the tie.

What are they searching for? I think it is to find the limit of the space.

Here is what I mean. The year Bobby was twenty, Bob and I went to Europe, leaving Bobby in charge of the house. Bob asked him to turn on the car every few days. He did not have permission to drive, however, since he was not insured. Bobby says that what happened was that he was late for an appointment. He looked at the time, looked at the car, looked at the time, and said, "Oh, well." Once he broke the rule, he couldn't stop driving. He put fifteen hundred miles on the car while we were gone, destroyed the muffler, lost the gas cap, and did other minor damage. We were horrified; after years of battling, it was more than we could take. Bobby remembers hiding under the covers when we found out about the car, hoping we wouldn't notice all 6 foot 4 inches of him huddled in the corner of his bed. Maybe, he thought, they'll just get over it. We didn't, and he left home. He fumbled around for a while—for a few days he even slept under the house—before finding his way.

When we hit that wall, I thought it was over, and I thought that I had failed. I had wanted so much to undo the pain of desertion that Bobby carried with him, and yet nothing I'd tried seemed to anchor him with me, with us, in a real world in which he was able to live showing concern for others. It was like something out of an old fairy tale, where the son is shoved out of the house, "and don't come back until you've made something of yourself!" I was slightly comforted by the idea that we were not the first parents to face such a situation, but it was thin comfort. When we hit a wall with Dina, and Kenny didn't graduate after five years of college, and Molly turned "bold," I thought surely I am the most failed mother ever put on the earth.

And then they all started to make something of themselves. As workers, parents, friends, lovers, they took on new roles and new duties, daring and succeeding. Suddenly, what emerges after all these years is a shared center. It wasn't that there could never be such a thing, it was just that we could not reach it quickly. There was a price to be paid and lessons to be learned before we could have something in common.

As for the boxcar—the boxcars, in our case—I would bet any amount of money that they're out back.

The boxcar, when it is no longer a refuge, becomes a treasure. The children made a home there, expressing their own urge to live. I do not know exactly what the boxcar looks like in adult life: is it solitary hobbies? daydreaming? retreat in the face of intimacy? acting out in the old troubled ways? We will see.

FIRST PLACE

One day soon Molly will find a beautiful thing. Something that a boy can't give her in a magic kiss. Something that an enchanted forest can't give to her in a song. But what I know, and what I think she knows, is that she already possesses this beautiful thing. She possesses the sun in her eyes. A moon in her belly. So, soon something beautiful will tickle her toes and swim through her teeth. It will see the sun in her eyes and say, "Molly, you moon-belly mama, you!" Molly swims space on street corners and sings rainbows in the sand. Molly hugs the sky. She hugs the sky with her shining moonbelly. Molly is a jolly wally.

Hannah Walcott
"Some Time Soon," 1996

Molly, my youngest child, was born during my first year of residency in psychiatry. I was in a session with a patient when the labor pains began. I made it through the session and the drive home, the hours of labor, and the cesarean section. Baby Molly smiled at me and I was in love. This moment of falling in love with a child has hit me with each of my children. It is always like a thunderclap. I fell in love with our son Kenny, who joined our family at age four, just as he entered the door of school to start kindergarten. He looked back at me with such terror in his eyes that I was overwhelmed with pain. I later asked a friend, "What is this agony I'm feeling?" "Oh, that," she said. "You've fallen in love with your son." "I didn't know it would feel like this," I said in wonder. "Oh yeah. And wait 'til they start to leave home. Then you'll really know worry."

The worry of children leaving home is not enough of a worry that you want to keep them home. It's not a 104°-fever worry, for example, or a *you-did-what?* worry. It is more a parting, a crossroads.

They go into a world you cannot enter. Maybe they send back little postcards, maybe they don't. You wait and hope. You cannot protect them. You cannot do it for them. That would defeat the whole point of separation. In fact, you should feel joyous that they've gone into the world. But, at least in my experience, you do and you don't. Part of you wants Baby back, right in front of you, where you can keep an eye out, make sure she's safe. Enough wallowing, though. They leave, you have to look happy, hope they write.

Molly decided, at twelve, that she was ready to go to camp. It is not unlike Molly that she came to this decision in May, when it was late to start searching for camps. There was the tension, typical of that era in family relations, between the camp her dad liked for her and the one I preferred. However, his camp never answered my phone calls, while mine had an August opening. When I told Molly that I'd signed her up for a camp that did a lot of hiking and canoeing, she looked at me aghast. Whatever had I been thinking? she wondered aloud. Hadn't I noticed that she didn't like dirt? Molly was prissy as a child. She liked to change her dress three or four times a day — and I do mean her dress — and she never, ever, played in the mud. If somehow a little dirt got on her hand, she came running into the house so someone could wash it off for her. This neat child was very nervous when the time came to go to the mountains. The morning she left, she shouldered the new backpack and gave me a withering look. Then she grabbed my hand, hers sweaty with fear. She was off to what?

Salt Ash Mountain, commonly known as SAM, is one of the five Farm and Wilderness (F&W) Camps founded in the 1930s by Ken and Susan Webb. I knew about these camps because I had been a baby-sitter at Tamarack Farm, the teen work camp, when I was fourteen. That same year, as well as the next, my brother Josh was a camper at Timberlake, the boys' camp. We both prospered there. In addition to those three camps there is Indian Brook for girls and Flying Cloud (FC) for boys who want to camp in a traditional Native American fashion.

I worked for a dance teacher, which meant that I took care of her young daughter in the mornings and played with the other campers in the afternoons. Needless to say, I came to like the afternoons better than the mornings. I was fortunate that an older counselor, Mary, who ran a nursery for all the little ones, babysat for *me* during those hours. As a respite or reward, the babysitting job allowed me to go on a weeklong hike across the mountains.

An important part of my Farm story is that I was ill-equipped for this venture. I borrowed some hiking boots that didn't fit, an ancient backpack that distributed weight so as to increase the poundage, and a threadbare sleeping bag. Off I went, little comprehending what I was getting myself into. It hit me at about the third mountain. I was in agony. I was astounded at how steep those old mountains were and how hard and cold they could be. But it was the fact that there was one mountain after another that did me in. I stood at the top of that awful rock and all I could see in any direction was wild, steep mountain. No roads, no cars, no helicopters, no Scotty to beam me up.

I was here. Out of "here" was "there." No matter how I sliced it, between me and "there" were mountains. There was no way out that did not involve climbing mountains. Tears, prayers, Scotty—none of that could save me.

I don't remember what I thought next, except that I knew I had to keep walking. As I walked, things got worse: the ill-fitting boots raised a massive blister on my heel. I shivered all through the nights in the threadbare sleeping bag. My shoulders ached from the pack I had to lug. The counselors, especially Margaret, whom I loved, worked hard to keep my lagging spirits up. The other campers were tender, as well. And, glory be, one day I slid down the last mountainside to the van that would carry us back to camp!

That moment surveying the endless terrain of mountains has burned in my brain for many years now. Whenever I discover that I have a long way to go to get "there," that moment in the mountains pops into my mind. It is the poignant moment on top of Mount Lafayette, watching the swirling fog and dreading the distance that lay ahead that I remember. I am reminded, from that experience, that I can go on.

I learned on that trip that my body could make it. I learned something about faith in others. I learned a lot about the darkest hour that comes just before the dawn. Because the body is the first place in which we live, we need to know its strengths and limits. We also need to learn to nourish the spirit that keeps the body moving. I sometimes thought that the best life-training I could give Molly was the chance to hike those mountains, to learn that she, too, could climb in and come out again.

So I sent Molly off to SAM, and sure enough, no sooner had she arrived than she set out with the other girls in her cabin on her first hike. Her first letter contained a minimal amount of information. "Hi, I'm having a good time at camp. I got back from my first hiking trip a few hours ago. It was good exercise and a lot of fun." The next trip was a six-day hiking trip. On her return, she wrote, "Camp is cool. Yesterday I returned from a 6-day hiking trip. The places we went were beautiful, but I was glad to run to camp."

I hoped that she had a good time. Bob and I drove up for the Camp Fair, an annual extravaganza homemade by the campers. The SAM booth sells the SAM-label root beer, known as SAM Dew. We were walking slowly across a muddy field when Molly spied us from the top of the fairgrounds. She came whooping down the hillside, bounding into our arms, hugging and kissing us with extraordinary joy. I was so happy to see her, and so happy that she was happy to see me, that I had to blink away the tears. Then I had to blink some more. My little Molly was dirty. Not a little dirty, but very dirty. She was, in fact, covered with mud. "We hiked down from SAM this morning, and it was rainy," she said blithely, dancing around on her bare and dirty feet. "Come meet my friends, come see everything."

Molly had hiked, Molly had played, Molly had gotten dirty. Molly was a new girl. Or almost new. A bit of the old timidity still clung to her. She would hike, but not the hardest mountains. She would play, but just some games.

The next year, Molly returned to SAM. She hiked, she milked a cow, she deepened old friendships and made new ones. She learned to endure. She wrote, "My cabin is OK. There are some cool people in it but some people fight with each other all the time. It was pretty bad for a little while but sometimes the fights are so stupid they just make you laugh!" She added a P.S.: "Don't worry, Mom. I'm perfectly fine." Later she described a six-day hiking trip: "My trip was what one would call a learning experience. There were a lot of people on the trip that drove me crazy, but what can you do about it?"

Parents read these snippets of information and try to create a vision of the world of camp. How ludicrous! The romances, the early-teen traumas are all carefully edited away, hinted at so obliquely that it would never cross the parent's mind, "Oh, *that's* what she meant!" But the tone of the letters is unmistakably different. Good and bad and managing make their appearance. There is a new quality of reflection that is welcome and exciting. This is a more mature Molly. She is beginning to expand a little, past the boundaries of her fears and her wants. She is taking Farm and Wilderness into her being.

F & W

Ken and Susan Webb, in developing F&W, brought together Quaker and Vermont traditions. The camps are designed to foster loving relationships with people and with nature. Farm and Wilderness wants to build community, foster brotherhood, and help people have fun. Joining with nature is woven through the fabric of the place. Other places I have visited attempt to civilize a bit of land, and that is where the cabins are erected. Nature is only present to provide cool breezes and a nice lake. That was not the Webbs' idea of how to build a camp. They attempted to hide the camp in the woods. Nature, in the form of bugs and trees and the elements, is everywhere at F&W. Though there are camp buildings of various sorts, at no point inside the buildings do you feel shut away from the trees and living creatures around you. Each cabin is set among the trees, hidden from all but the initiates. The cabins are semistructured, intended to let in, rather than keep out, air and light and wind. The outhouses, called kybos, were transformed from ordinary smelly structures into rooms with views. The better the view, the more valued the kybo. Some of the F&W kybos look out over lakes, others over mountains. Most are made for three or four people, which introduces communal living to the toilet.

The camps are sited on a series of beautiful lakes. Ken and Susan believed heartily in the Vermont tradition of skinny-dipping. Few wear bathing suits at camp. The focus is not on suits but on enduring the cold water. The truly hearty people are up at dawn for an eye-opening dip. Their splashes ring before the meal bells, telling the less courageous that a new day is calling. Those same hearty types are often off for a walk of several miles, or a jog up a steep hill. They set a high standard of joining the outdoors. The citified folk follow, timidly at first, but more or less joyously as they get used to it. "You go *into* nature," Molly says. "If I hadn't gone to SAM I might have thought that nature was scary. I might have been afraid of dirt. I might not have learned the things I know about myself."

The *Farm* part in F&W has to do with tending the land and its creatures. The farming is in the traditions of Vermont. It is faithful to local practice in its awareness of the place and what farming means to the people. A young farmer, who lived near F&W, was having a hard year. His wife was ill, and he was afraid he would lose his crops because he was behind in his work. A group from F&W went up and worked for a day, weeding and tending, lending a hand to a fellow farmer having a patch of trouble. F&W farms out of concern for the Earth and love of feeding people. It is an antichemical, pro-food kind of activity. It is customary, in late summer, to see people returning from the farms with bunches of carrots just pulled out of the ground and covered with bits of earth. It is hearty food one eats there: fresh baked bread and pancakes and just-picked vegetables.

The *Wilderness* in F&W has to do with going out into the mountains and rivers and lakes to see what is there. Vermont, New Hampshire, and Maine are lightly peopled. There is still wilderness right at one's doorstep. It is possible to hike through the mountains to make the trip from SAM to the main camps several miles away. A trip in a van takes campers to the deeper wilderness of the White Mountains in New Hampshire or remote areas of Maine where there are adventures to be had, moose to be seen, challenges to be overcome.

Spirituality, loosely defined, keeps it all going. Following the basic structure of Quaker Meeting, in which people speak when they are moved by the Spirit, campers and their counselors gather once a day. Meetings are held close to nature; campers and their counselors sit in a circle. Counselors and older campers model for newcomers the communion with the Spirit. Comments might dwell on the simple beauty of an emerald green snake, or the process of getting to know new friends. There is no a priori rule about what might be said: what is said is what one is moved to say. The words, in a sense, belong to the Spirit, and the speaker is simply the mouthpiece of the eternal, the universal, the all-encompassing, of which we are each a part. I feel the Great Spirit as a force encircling me—God constantly at my back—and this feeling flows from the daily Meetings that summer I spent at Tamarack Farm.

God is all around in an outdoor circle like that. Black Elk, a spiritual leader of the Sioux Indians who fought against Custer at Little Big Horn, was most perplexed by the white man's habit of living in square houses. Life, itself a cycle of birth and death and new life, should be lived in a circle, just as a teepee was a circle, and teepees were placed in a circle. A circle had freedom, whereas sharp edges were antilife. He described coming to live on the reservation after his tribe was defeated by the U.S. Army:

we made these little gray houses of logs that you see, and they are square. It is a bad way to live, for there can be no power in a square.

You have noticed that everything an Indian does is in a circle, and that is because the Power of the World always works in circles, and everything tries to be round. In the old days when we were a strong and happy people, all our power came to us from the sacred hoop of the nation, and so long as the hoop was unbroken, the people flourished. . . . Everything the Power of the World does is done in a circle. The sky is round, and I have heard that the earth is round like a ball, and so are all the stars. The wind, in its greatest power, whirls. Birds make their nests in circles, for theirs is the same religion as ours. The sun comes forth and goes down in a circle. The moon does the same, and both are round. Even the seasons form a great circle in their changing, and always come back again to where they were. The life of a man is a circle from childhood to childhood, and so it is in everything where power moves.[1]

At SAM the circle for Meeting sits at the top of a hill, overlooking a beautiful lake. Members of the community sit on logs or lounge on the grass, often entwining themselves with each other. As hard as it seems to be for young teenagers to be reflective and sentimental in a public setting, that is what they are asked to do. Part of the bond that develops at camp is the connection formed in the intimacy of Meeting. Molly describes it as "a perfect place." To speak the truth was the point of Meeting. Gabe, a good friend, said at the opening of camp Molly's last summer, "I look around the circle and I see so many people I don't know. But I look forward to getting to know you. And I know that by the time I leave here at the end of the summer, you'll all be really good friends." These words rang throughout the summer for Molly: in fact, the truth Gabe uttered seemed to describe the process of SAM, strangers transformed into deeply loved friends. The spiritual connections that had so nurtured her in her first two seasons at camp were essential to the transformation she made in her third.

BECOMING

The letters home were remarkably better that third summer. Molly had developed a witty style of commentary and a point of view, often a rather cynical one. In her first letter, she wrote, "Camp is good. I'm having a really great time. We got back from our cabin trips yesterday. My cabin trip was interesting. There wasn't too much hiking involved. We had to use compasses and maps to find this gold mine thing. When we finally found it, it was just a pile of rocks. Yeah, the excitement was never ending." She went on with a lively story about a girl who was obsessed with animal rights and refused to kill "mesquitos"! (She claimed later that she spelled it that way on purpose. She did not say *what* purpose.)

Soon after, she wrote, "I think I'm going to be on the hardest hiking trip for my next trip. What's up with you requesting [on a parents' questionnaire] that I be challenged? They took your request very seriously. I'm sort of looking forward to a hard trip though. It'll feel good to know that I did it." That first challenging trip was to the White Mountains. She wrote, "I just got back from the White Mountains in New Hampshire. It is one of the two hardest trips of all of the hiking trips SAM does. Can you imagine that? *Me* on one of the hardest hiking trips. I was pretty impressed by myself. Of course, there were times when I swore that when that trip was over, if I ever saw a mountain again, I might get violent. The hiking was really hard but the views were amazing and it was worth it. It was one of the best trips I've ever been on."

SAM, at the end of each of the two camp sessions, July and August, has a banquet accompanied by a ceremonial tradition called Appreciations. Each member of the community takes responsibility for appreciating one other member, through a gift and small speech. Molly wrote, "One of my really good friends, Gabe (he's gone now he was only here first [session]), had me for appreciations. He made me a really cool quilty-thing. It was great because I didn't know he had me. Michelle (the director of the camp) spoke about me. She said really nice things. I was kind of honored that she spoke about me because she always only talks about one camper. I hope that I've told you about appreciations before so that you know what I'm talking about. If I haven't told you about it I'll explain in my next letter."

Michelle later told me that, at that particular Appreciations gathering, she had told how moved she was to watch Molly take on the White Mountain trip. She had urged Molly to push herself, and Molly had taken up—and met—the challenge. Hiking a big mountain requires little more than putting one foot in front of the other and a lot of heart. What Molly showed was that she had heart. From the timid little girl, afraid to get dirty, to the articulate young mountain climber, she had shown many new sides of herself to the world.

The second half of the summer Molly went on another challenging trip to Flagstaff, Maine, which included several days of canoeing and several days of challenging hiking. The trip is divided so that some campers canoe while others hike. For Molly, the canoeing came first. She remembers the mountains looming overhead and thinking, "Wow—I have to climb those mountains. I can still picture the mountain rising over the lake." The hiking was every bit as hard as she had thought it would be, but not harder than what she could manage. Her joy as she reached the top was overwhelming. She nearly ran to the top, just to be there. "I know now, that when things get hard, I'll remember that I did Flagstaff."

Molly thought about what she was doing on several levels. She was pushing herself physically and mentally. But she was also finding who she was as a person. Flying Cloud is the boys' F&W camp designed on the ways and teachings of Native Americans. There, people live in teepees and try to understand the circles of life. One of the ceremonies of Flying Cloud, Molly wrote, is a Wachipi. "I just got back from my cabinwork trip. It was a lot of fun. Rachel and Delia were on the trip with me. On the first night of our trip we got to go to a Wachipi. This kid I know named Cody got named. His FC name is Sunrise Cougar. I think that that is a great name. The Wachipi was alot of fun. I love Wachipis (not just because I get to see FC). After the Wachipi we spent the night at Flying Cloud. That was a nice experience. Sometimes I wish that there were an FC for girls. I would love to get an FC name." An FC name, as in Native American naming traditions, was a symbol of something characteristic of the person. It was not a superficial characteristic, however, but a naming of the way the person's spirit moved in the world. Sunrise Cougar.

Molly longed to know her spirit by having loved ones name it for her. She talked often about the idea of FC for girls. In fact, she planned to be the director of it when it was opened. Apparently, such a camp has been discussed at F&W but has never materialized. Molly was ready for it to come into being. Then, she would be named and she would know who she was. Who she *really* was, underneath the growing and changing, the constant self that would meet with the universe. Molly-Who-Flies-To-The-Mountain-Top, I thought. Mountain Dove.

In a way, Molly seemed very much to have found herself at camp. She is a powerful young woman, and she was a leader at camp. Skits are a big part of life at SAM. There are skits after each of the trips, and there are skits when the camps get together. Molly was intensely competitive about these skits. She was really offended if the SAM skit was corny. "Samrassic Park" earned her contempt, for example. She spent hours writing and perfecting various scripts and expected others to like them as much as she did. She took to singing and often led others in singing. In her third year, she was one of the chore assistants and had to report on the way that chores were performed. She was the China Drone, which meant that she had a special bucket-hat complete with decorative forks to wear at after-meal gatherings.

She would award praise or blame, as the occasion demanded. She had a blithe way of scolding people that seemed likely to make a point without alienating friends, and she kept it at that. She says that being China Drone involved showing up at meals. Molly does show up for meals.

Another sign that Molly had found herself was in her growing interest in solo trips. Solos, time spent alone in the forest, were frightening to her at first. The camp helps young people adjust to the challenge of the solo by sending them out for an hour at first and for longer periods of time as they adjust to solitude. Molly came to love the time alone. "I never brought a book. It didn't seem right. I wanted to be there, in the woods, listening and thinking." Molly is a chatterbox and very sociable. As a little child, she used to install herself at the kitchen table and eat breakfast with every member of the family as they came through. She got a lot of breakfasts, and a lot of visits just hanging out. "Molly alone" doesn't ring a bell for those who know her. It was a part that she found or learned or met while at SAM.

Molly says that, during the school year, when she was angry with school, she would remind herself that summer was coming and she could go back to SAM, a place where she knew she belonged, a place where she was happy. When she reached fourteen, and her last summer at SAM, she faced the certain loss of that place to be Molly. She cried a lot during the last month of camp and hugged people incessantly. Molly was a big fan of group hugs. SAM went on, for her, in the friendships she had made. It also went on through the pleasant tradition of Work Weekends, a chance for the extended family of F&W to return and take care of the camps by repairing and painting and doing odd jobs. The Work Weekends put the camps to bed in the fall and woke them up each spring. Molly went often with Rachel or Delia. I could not picture that they did any work—too busy hugging. "Work?" she would ask me. "We're teenagers." I'm not sure what that meant, but that's what she said.

F&W leaves a powerful imprint on people. Martha, my dear friend from medical school, had been a counselor at Indian Brook, the camp for girls. Later, she sent her children to F&W. Finally, she moved herself and her family to Vermont. She has deep family roots in

Vermont that coupled with the pull of the place she felt as a counselor. I have a truly glorious picture of Martha holding a monstrous pig and grinning from ear to ear. She rarely grinned like that when we were at the Columbia University College of Physicians and Surgeons. She seemed, often, a step, or a half step, off the beat, as if we were all marching to some tune, but she didn't get the rhythm. Back in Vermont, she gets the rhythm. Slow, measured, comfortable. She is the very image of a country doctor. Her patients are her neighbors. If she gets a page on her beeper while walking her dog through the little town where she lives, she can knock on any door to ask to use the phone. Everything about it pleases her, fits. It is, in part, the F&W effect.

I notice it in Molly, and I have more than a touch of it myself. Shoes, for example. Having walked with my feet in touch with the earth, I felt no need to wear shoes ever again. In the depth of winter, my father used to say to me, "If you'd wear socks, you wouldn't get so many colds." I didn't like the colds, but I wanted to feel the soil, and the rocks, the heat and wet of the earth wherever I went. My freshman year at Bryn Mawr College, I walked on warm floors. I thought that must really be what wealth was about: no need to wear shoes inside in the winter because the floors were so roasty toasty warm. F&W shows up in clothes, too. Jeans and bandanas, long, flowing skirts, are Molly's uniforms. I once thought that there would never be a time in my life when I wouldn't wear jeans. I couldn't imagine dress clothes as a way of life. I still can't. I've tried to find some compromises that come close to, but do not cross, the line of formality. Molly does not yet concede even that.

One lovely spring day, Molly and Delia describe for me the last night they were together at SAM. They stayed up all night. As the sun rose over the lake, they thought there must be something they hadn't done yet. Delia said, "Let's roll down the hill." So they rolled down the dew-soaked hill that sloped to lakefront, getting dirty and wet and laughing all the way down. Somewhere down around the middle of the hill, Molly remembered that she had to wear her clothes all the way home on the bus to New York. But it didn't matter. Then they sat on the hill and sang camp songs until the sun rose over the lake. Searching for those rituals of women that might ease their transition, lacking the connection to the ancient traditions that FC gave boys, they invented their own ways of bonding and of letting go.

As the end of the last meal drew near, and people started to clear the table, Molly announced, "If we don't finish breakfast, camp won't be over. So let's eat very slowly. I refuse to finish. Leave my breakfast." Her obstinance did not slow the inevitable close of the summer. Entering New York City, watching the pollution fill the sky and buildings close in on the horizon, she was horrified. She reflects, "You know, you pretend you miss things at home, like TV and pizza and showers, but you don't, really. You just want to be back at camp."

HOMESTEADING

In filtered light
"Want your coffee
in there?"
"Please."
Steamy greeting
mug
to hand.
Yellow truck
coughs. Sun
glinting
in the window.
"We haven't had
artichokes
in ages."
Knowing that
the best blueberries
lurk deeper in
the woods
than they
are willing
to go, I go.
"Why?" you ask,
pondering
artichokes
and blueberries.

*

Honking bus.
Truck coughs again.
Coffee has
spent its
hot good
morning
in filtered
light.

Mindy Thompson
"In Filtered Light," 1982

On October 17, 1989, at 5:17 P.M., an earthquake measuring 7.0 on the Richter scale shook the San Francisco Bay area. Bob and I were in our office at 74 New Montgomery Street, an older office building that rattled back and forth. We were shaken to our knees, and I thought, "If this doesn't stop, the building will fall down and we'll all be dead." A profound sense of helplessness filled me as the building continued to sway.

All of us were confused about what to do next when the quake finally ended. A young man from another part of the building came up to our floor with a flashlight. "We have to get out," he said. "There's structural damage to the building." That decided the matter, and we rushed out, grateful for his leadership and also his flashlight, since some of the stairs were blocked and the emergency lights didn't work.

On the street, thousands of people milled around listening to radios and looking up at the sky to see if glass was falling. BART, the light-rail system, was out. The Bay Bridge was broken. Bob and I had no easy way to get home. For once, I had a lot of money in my pocket, and it was strange to think that it wasn't worth anything. I couldn't rent a car, for example, because the computers were down. I couldn't go to a hotel: they, too, had no electricity.

We slowly made our way to the Civic Center, which is built like a spaceship and rests on giant springs. In case of an earthquake it would simply bob up and down. Or so I believed that night. It seemed by far the safest place to be. The Red Cross brought food, blankets, and beds for the crowd that straggled in through the night. Many there were homeless people who based themselves in the area. Some had been my patients when I worked in the Tenderloin area of San Francisco. Those folks all came by to say, "Hey, Dr. Fullilove, how you doin'?" It was good to see friendly faces.

The night passed slowly. In the weeks prior to the earthquake, Bob and I had decided to move back to the East Coast and live in Manhattan. But in the dark, chilly hours of the night, all I could think about was Lady Jane's Restaurant in Hoboken, New Jersey. My mother had moved to Hoboken a few years before. We had stayed with her while arranging for our new jobs and housing. She had first taken us to Lady Jane's, and we loved the grand wooden bar and the large windows overlooking the Empire State Building. It was a Berkeley kind of place in a Jersey mode. At about 1 A.M. Lady Jane's took on a magical quality. Back in San Francisco's Civic Center, I counted the minutes until six o'clock, when I could call my mother. "Mom, we want to live in Hoboken. Find us a place." And that is how we came home to New Jersey.

If Newark were still standing—or if East Orange had continued to be one of the most livable cities in America—I think our homecoming would have taken us in that direction. But the destruction of that area is so advanced that there didn't seem to be any "home" left there. Hudson County was once again a Thompson outpost, having been resettled by my mom after forty years in Orange. Bob and I began our homesteading effort by looking for a house.

THE BIG HOUSE

I have always dreamed of a big house, a house like 10 South Maple Avenue. This dream of a big house echoes through time and place in the lives of other people. Elizabeth White, born in 1892 in the Hopi village of Old Oraibi, remembered a night when the rain had passed but the drops, falling through the leaky roof of the family's one-room house, had soaked the floor. She went outside and warmed her feet with the ashes of her mother's cook fire. The clouds passed and the stars came out. Looking at them, she hoped that someday she might understand the meaning of the bright holes in the sky, opening to some unknown world.

> And then I thought of the folks in the house and I thought if we had a bigger home there'd be room for all of us and maybe it wouldn't leak like it did. And all these childish thoughts went through my head. "And with that mysterious thing up above," I said to myself, "when I grow up I'll understand. And when I grow up I'm going to build a big home, a very large home, big enough for my whole family, my relatives."
>
> You know how a child dreams. That was my childhood dream that developed there. Little did I know that this was a mysterious dream, because when I left from there on any little thing that was of value, I always thought, "Maybe I will think of the future connected with it." [1]

Elizabeth White became an artist and a teacher. She built a big house to shelter her family. In her seventies she faced the devastating experience of losing her big house to fire. Even though she rebuilt it, the memory of that time was cloaked in pain. If the dream of the big house had been a link to the future, perhaps the loss of the house was a signal of the end, or something worse. "I can't talk about that time—I don't understand it yet," she said.

Mariana, a woman with AIDS living in New York City and unaware of Elizabeth White or her childhood dream of a big house, had nearly the same fantasy. She feared what would happen to her children when she died. "It would be good if we got a big building, an apartment building, and then all the children could live there together," she said, reflecting on the problem.

Angie, a young girl living in a welfare hotel for homeless families, said nearly the same thing. "I wish someone in New York could help us. Put all of the money that we have together and we buy a building. Two or three rooms for every family. Everybody have a kitchen." [2]

In these dreams of a big house, the house is more than shelter. It permits safety and togetherness. The upheavals and fears that come from houselessness are eliminated. Stability and kindness take their place. In the dream of the big house, things are better, because people have room in which to work out their relationships. There is space for relatedness to blossom. Some kinds of space seem particularly designed to nourish souls.

I had, myself, managed to live in two big houses. The first, in Englewood, is the house my children dream of reacquiring. The second, in Berkeley, is the house Bob considers his favorite. What we had tried to create in that house was the embodiment of a dream of comfort that we had envisioned at the beginning of our relationship in 1982. Bob had put the dream into drawings, while I had expressed it in poetry.

When I moved to Hoboken, I imagined that I would find a new big house to help us realize our imaginings. Not so. Hoboken is a townhouse place. Here, the houses are tall and thin, and we live in one of those houses.

NOT BIG, THIN

Our thin house is not a big house, and the challenge has been to create a refreshing life in tight quarters. The layout is that of three small boxes, laid one on top of the other. I think of them as layers of the forest, each a kind of niche in the ecosystem, a layer of the world, supporting different kinds of life. The lower world, the Earth layer, is where we have the kitchen-dining-Bob's work-TV area, which is filled with lots of stuff. It is a lot to tuck into a small room, but those spaces can't be separated because of certain spatial rules. My rule is that the kitchen has to look out over the garden. Bob's rule is that he should be able to wander from his computer to the stew pot to the television as he putters away the day.

When we first moved to the house, we lived in an awful state. Little did I realize that the lovely, wide floorboards with country farmhouse appeal were far enough apart that the wind could whistle through the house. Through the winter of 1994, when there were eighteen snowstorms and sixteen freeze-thaw cycles, the temperature in the house hovered at 55 degrees. We were cold and unhappy. At other times of the year, a leak beneath the bottom floor created a smelly pool of water that served as a breeding pond for bugs.

Finally, the only bathroom was all the way up on the third floor, which seemed very far away from everything. Bob would sit in the kitchen and moan, "I hate this house, I hate this house, I can't bear this house." Molly would say things like, "Can't you fix this, Mom?" I would ask myself, "Do I *really* have to go to the bathroom *now?*"

A major transformation of that first layer took place under the watchful leadership of architect Joe Vitullo. Joe, who was in his early sixties when we first met him, was a short, dapper, bulldog-looking guy with a tendency to be dramatic. He came to see us, looked around, got a stern look in his eye, and pronounced, "I'm going to have to prescribe serious medicine for this house." Then he left.

It was months before we could get him back. "I don't like working with doctors," he complained, looking accusingly at me. He forgave us because we weren't *technicians*—we were *scholars*. Part of him longed for the academic life we led. "You *read!*" he exclaimed. "Do you know what it's like for me surrounded all day by *peons!* They don't *read!* You *read!*" When I showed him my books on the psychology of place, he was consumed with envy. How could it be that a *doctor* could be reading such wonderful *architecture* books? He forgave us again. It went on like that.

Finally Joe prescribed the medicine, but it was too strong for us. The general contractor, Mauro, bailed us out. Joe was hardly forgiving. "You let a *carpenter* ruin my ideas," was his assessment, his voice dripping with contempt. I think he was pleased with the big table that served as dining–work space–stuff attractor. But when his eye, roving over the first floor, caught sight of the back door, a shudder went through his body. "If I'm to help you," he said, "that door MUST GO. A *carpenter* made that door." Absolution for the low, low price of a better door. Silver, our foster cat, really likes the door because he can sit before it and look at the birds in the garden.

The second layer of the house-system is at the level of the top of the cherry tree. It has high ceilings, long windows that let in the light, and floor-to-ceiling bookcases. This middle world has had a number of lives in the short time we've been in the house. It housed my brother Josh for a year, then Kenny stayed for two years. It was All-We-Had during three months of remodeling, which left a bad taste for the whole floor in the minds of Molly and Bob. I used to wonder why Josh and Kenny stayed as long as they did under what seemed to me cramped conditions. When I moved my desk into the back room, I discovered that it is a quiet eddy off from the swirl of the house. One can think deep thoughts in that room.

The top of the house-system, which looks out into the top branches of the neighbor's oak tree, has two bedrooms and a bathroom. Molly's bedroom is in the front. It has original Hoboken ceilings and wallpaper, but her friends have added some postmodern touches. During her senior year in high school, she threw out all her furniture and got new things. "It's the place story of my life," she told me. "I'll tell you some time."

Bob and I are in the back, in the room with the skylight. It is bright very early in the morning, and the moon shines in at night. I feel the snow before I see it, because it covers the skylight, darkening the room. The ceiling is so high it takes a tall ladder to change the lightbulbs. It is an aerie as opposed to a cave: nothing could be more opposite to the feeling of the first floor, for the upper world is heavenly, whereas the lower world is cavelike.

The fourth part of our house is the garden. Hoboken gardens are usually behind the houses. Because the houses are set side by side, enclosing the block, the gardens are hidden. Passersby on the street might be able to tell if your house is tidy, but they can't see your garden at all. On our block, the ring of houses creates an island, which is divided into our gardens. Years ago, there were no fences, so children could run from house to house in this interior yard. But that level of intimacy among the families has disappeared. By the time we moved in, every yard was fenced off from every other yard. Running in a row down the middle of the interior are sheds of every description. We have several big trees in our courtyard, and for a long while, Silver was the only cat in the neighborhood, so birds delighted in this arrangement and chattered about all day long.

Three worlds and a garden define our house. Our thin—fifteen feet wide, to be exact—house is a vast difference from 10 S. Maple Avenue and from our house in Berkeley. Adjusting to thin has been hard. We tried simple tricks, like compressing our minds so they wouldn't hit the walls, but this just made us long for more space. We tried, as well, to ponder the ecological benefits of a small house. With all of America going mad for square footage, we were doing the right thing in our thin house. This was not comforting, either.

Part of my study of the psychology of place has been to observe the changes that follow simple alterations in the placement of objects. I have had a number of stunning experiences of how this works. One such experience was the alteration of our workplace by an Adopt-a-Space campaign. The campaign arose out of my disgust with coffee grounds and grease left in the common sink. In the no-man's-land of the kitchen, the thirty people who worked on the floor showed a startling disregard for cleanliness. A high school student, Maureen Turner, pointed out that the problem was much bigger than the kitchen: every common space was used as a dumping ground. The Adopt-a-Space campaign assigned ownership for these areas and abruptly altered the pattern of neglect. My coworkers brought taste and style to their efforts. Each space became more lively and more charming. Adrian Birt was particularly skillful at creating setting. Under her direction, the addition of plants, a mirror, and a fish tank transformed an oppressive, windowless conference room into a sought-after meeting place.

Another important experience of transformation occurred at Amanda's, a well-known Hoboken restaurant. When the restaurant first opened, Bob and I went several times. I noticed that we always argued while eating there, and we transferred our trade to other local establishments. When new management took over, we went back and had a completely different experience. The place now offered intimate dining, rather than an occasion for rancour. As I got to know the owner, Eugene Flynn, I shared my experience of the place and asked what he had done to re-create the place.

The first few times I asked, he described the changes in lighting, the practice of greeting people at the door, and the staff's alertness to diners' needs. As he got to know me better, he quipped, "Maybe it's because we don't have glass tops over the tablecloths, and nobody sprays Windex while you're eating!" Hey, that could be it.

Adrian and Eugene inspired me with their remarkable capacity to create setting. But I didn't notice that any of my own efforts were creating that kind of calm and charm at home.

I was close to desperate when I met by chance Cary Medwin, a feng shui expert who was helping my friend David Jenkins adjust to life in a single-room occupancy hotel. I had visited David's home enough to appreciate the changes he had made under her direction. I immediately asked if she would help us manage the thin house.

Feng shui is an ancient Chinese system of creating harmonious surroundings that bring happiness, prosperity, and good health. Man-Ho Kwok notes, "At the heart of feng shui is the desire to acknowledge the power of the natural world and to live in harmony with it."[3] Feng shui is a science that guides the shape and placement of objects to improve the flow of ch'i. Such a consultation is, Cary explained to us, the sharing of religious knowledge. This knowledge was not meant for everyone, only those ready to listen. The payment for the consultation was to be placed in nine red envelopes. Bob was drawn to this event. Although typically unwilling to discuss the house, he was eager to participate that afternoon.

Cary came early one Sunday afternoon, bringing with her a student. She was a little late because she had trouble finding us. People often have trouble finding their way into Hoboken. She described it as a very yin place because of the way it narrows and closes in. "Opportunity will have a hard time finding you," she pointed out.

The feeling of confusion—where do we go? where do we start?—became a dominant theme of the consultation. She asked to start at the front door. We have two doors to the front: a formal door that we never use, and an informal door to the lower world that we use all the time. "Which is the front door?" we asked.

She chuckled and turned to her student. "Isn't that interesting? You had asked exactly that question even before we got here! You're very attuned to the process." Cary explained to us that the front door was the formal door, and so we went to look at that door. She recommended that we use that door more, since it would open the way for opportunity to find us. Wind chimes would be good, too, she pointed out, since the sound would draw us to the door.

Cary was most concerned about the number of books on the middle floor. "Books hold energy," she said. "You should get rid of the books." Books, according to Cary, send out needles, which are not good. The "attic" that I had constructed of bookcases and a dresser came in for similar censure: "It blocks the flow of energy from the front to the back." No books? No pseudo-attic? This was difficult to take. At about this time, the student turned to me and said, "Where will you put the books until you can get rid of them?" Clearly not a book person.

Cary liked the lower world for its openness and relative lack of books. She thought the big table was too rigid and hierarchical and the kitchen too small. "You feel cramped in here." Bob felt understood. We went to the third floor. In our room, she pointed out that the placement of the bed by the fireplace created a kind of insecurity. And the open closets, she thought, were not peaceful.

Molly's room Cary found perfect: lots of open space and all the objects arranged in the appropriate locations. Cary explained to us what she called the Bak Wa, that is the underlying structure of a room. For example, there is in every room a relationship area, a religion and spirituality area, a wealth area, and a creativity area. The placement of objects in the appropriate areas enhances the flow of ch'i in the room.

We talked of many things. She urged us to move, since she thought the thin house was not auspicious. If we couldn't move, perhaps the kitchen could be shifted to the middle floor to take advantage of the lovely space in the back of the house. She noted that we had put things in front of all six of the fireplaces, which definitely was blocking the flow of energy. And clutter. The explosion of stuff that had encroached on every inch of space was bad for the ch'i of the house.

Bob said to Cary in conclusion, "I'm just glad to know that I'm not crazy for hating this house."

After Cary had gone, he insisted we get to work immediately by moving the furniture in our bedroom. We slept that night against the stability of the south wall. It was a delightful change. Some of the advice was not so easy to follow. I immediately called my friends Francine Rainone and Fumiyo Akazawa, both osteopathic physicians who had studied in China. "Must I get rid of my books?" I asked.

They had many encouraging things to say. "Books are wonderful," Francine insisted. "Books bring you the world. Books that are opened release energy." Of course, not all books *are* opened: *those* could go. Fumiyo added a piece of advice that comforted me as the slow process of reordering the house went forward: "The house gods are very patient," she said. "You have a year or so to work on this."

Bob and I talked a lot about moving. Cary's nudge in that direction fired up all my wishes for a big house and all his hopes to be out of our little cubbyhole. The real estate market in Hoboken was hot: we could have sold our little place in a week. We kicked these ideas around for a while, but then the excitement about a new house evaporated.

One day at Lady Jane's Bob recounted for the nth time how much the place meant to us. Nicole Amato, who was our waitress that night, replied, "Well, we like you, too." She walked away and came back with a drink menu. In the upper right-hand corner it offered patrons the "Dr. Full-o-Love: Chamborde and champagne."

"I can never leave Hoboken," Bob concluded, shaking his head.

We couldn't leave Hoboken because of Eugene Flynn and his funny stories, because we would miss our Hudson School friends, because when we gave a Christmas Cookie Party our neighbors came, because it's only twenty minutes to work, because it's an old town finding new life, because my mother's here and my dad used to organize here, because Phil at the liquor store always has a great new wine, because our cherry tree is amazing in the spring, because Janet and Susan are the best Weight Watchers leaders in America, because the bread and the mozzarella are amazing, because of the saints' processions that come by the house, because the mailman is great, because we would miss Annie at the Court Street Restaurant, because, in sum, Hoboken works . . .

That says a lot. We'd been so oppressed by the stuck energy of the thin house that we'd forgotten to notice how much is working. We got pulled across the continent to this little town, this birthplace of Frank Sinatra, this home of baseball, this site of the first order for Oreo cookies. We landed, we struggled, we made a place, and then Lady Jane's christened champagne and Chamborde the "Dr. Full-o-Love."

In all the books *I've* read about homesteading, that's the point at which Paw turns to Maw and says, "Honey, this land is *our* land, now."

CONCLUSION

It is important, in closing, to talk about tomatoes. My dad learned farming from his dad. I learned a bit from him. I took over growing tomatoes the year he became too ill to garden. I have grown tomatoes ever since. Especially when I dig in Jersey soil, I feel that time has no boundaries and the Earth and I are one. My family has struggled to survive and flourish. I hope that, whatever success we attain, some of my children and grandchildren will always grow tomatoes. There is nothing quite like the moment when you pick a bright red, sun-warmed fruit from the vine and bite into it. To feel that is to feel life.

When I was eight and nine I went to a camp on Martha's Vineyard run by Phyllis Velasquez, who was known as Mrs. Val. She was a native of the island and a member of the local tribe. That gave her access to the clay cliffs and other areas that were the lands of her people. She took us everywhere on the island and taught us the traditional skills of fishing and clamming and crabbing. She taught us, as well, the roadside arts of painting scenes on clam shells and making braided rugs. She taught us to revel in the sun and the sea. She scoffed at the idea of showering after being in the ocean. "White people don't understand that you need the salt on your skin." She taught us not to be afraid of ticks or scissors bugs or emptying a cesspool. Life could only hurt us if we stayed away from it. Her lessons were always delicious, since they always ended in eating: corn fritters or blueberry pie or fried clams. Every once in a while, when I called home, I would ask my dad, "How are the tomatoes doing?" "Not ready, yet," he would say. We didn't have much to say to each other, but I was always heartened to know that the tomatoes would be waiting.

The objects of our longing, by necessity and by choice, are arrayed near and far, creating a life geography. At certain moments, the constellations of people and place exert such a powerful pull on the individual that the shape of the constellation is imprinted in character. It is the long shadow of such a moment that creates a psychology of place. An infant, left untended in a hospital, may never recover from that period of abandonment. An adult lost in the woods will carry the uncertainty of that episode. A political leader, forced into exile, will thereafter live two lives. The imprint of the constellated past can be traced in odd habits and behaviors, many of which are completely unconscious for the actor. I remodeled two houses to place the kitchen over the garden before I realized that that was the shape of my childhood home. My father often stood at the kitchen window watching his tomatoes grow and meditating on the future. I wanted to situate myself so that I might see the world as he saw it.

During his lifetime there was very little of such sharing. In fact, our situations following the 1957 school fight were so different that there was no reconciling our different points of view. The school fight was a signal victory for my dad but a terrible defeat for me. Though victory and defeat were both valid outcomes, only one outcome — victory — was ever acknowledged. My dad, good as he was at many things, was not good at accepting alternative points of view. He knew a single truth, and it wasn't mine. That made for many years of bitterness as I struggled to survive the hell of my displacement. The denial of my reality was nearly deadly for me. I was lucky to be given a second chance to restore the internal places that hurt so badly and to begin to live again.

It is as an adult psychiatrist that I can finally claim my own reality. But I would never suggest that my reality was the singular truth or that my reality should blot out my father's triumph. Victory and defeat are both truth, depending on one's perspective. An even more accurate way of understanding multiple truths is to understand that places exist at multiple level scales. My dad's truth was a political truth; it reflected the larger scales of group life. Even I would argue that I was a beneficiary of the freedom of movement he won for me. My pain, on the other hand, existed at the level of me, the individual. It was a personal truth of the self, which is the first place for all of us.

Dad's failure represents a type of error we are all likely to make.

I failed in exactly the same way with my second husband as he immersed himself in the study of French. I could not see his perspective. I lived only my own terror of losing him and had no access to his joy of learning.

Difficult situations—retreat, immersion, abandonment are but a few—represent the extreme pull of events on individual lives. However hard the individual struggles to balance the forces in play, it is unlikely that all parties will emerge satisfied. Was I satisfied with my mother's devotion? Were my children content to have been adopted? The first answer is no, but the final answer depends on our ability to see the situation through. It is the long tail of the situation that is so important. None of the stories I have related is finished; we keep changing the story by sharing and understanding.

One of the most important discoveries that I made while writing this book was how important it was for our family to have a common language for these difficult situations. My son Bobby often says to me, "Yeah, Mom, I read the book," as a shorthand for the exchange of confidences that the reading entailed.

I proposed, at the outset, that it is useful for psychiatry to have a language for situations, just as we have a language for emotions, behaviors, and thoughts. Through the structure of this book, I have tried to suggest that the language of situations includes, at a minimum, situation words, first-person accounts, place stories, and location inventories. It is not hard to work with these materials, once they have been shared.

I have most appreciated the discovery that differing perspectives need not be a source of discontent or enmity. Once perspectives are shared, the way is opened for three delightful emotions: tolerance, tenderness, and joy! I used to have a Native American roadside art plaque that read, "Do not judge another man until you have walked a mile in his moccasins." That made great sense to me, but I was not at all clear how this was to be accomplished. What pleases me is that the sharing of situations is a powerful way of "walking in another's moccasins."

I want to go back to tomatoes to make another point about the psychology of place, a point about belonging. My dad was greatly comforted by his garden. He missed the cycle of the seasons that he had learned at home. He had turned resolutely away from the life of the countryside because he could not tolerate the fear and the powerlessness. Two years before his death he visited his sister's house—the house of Joshua—and discovered that fear still reigned in the countryside. This was agony to him. He could not go home. Yet he missed the peaches and the asparagus that thrived in the hot summer days of Maryland and always thought of himself as a "homeboy" from the Eastern Shore. What did prosper in New Jersey were tomatoes, and therefore he stood at the window to watch the sweet fruit ripen and redden in our backyard.

Nearly a hundred years ago, W. E. B. Du Bois wrote that the problem of the color line would be the problem of the twentieth century. *Color line* has such a benign ring to it, I think. But the abuse that attended segregation was what drove Dad from his home and prevented him from returning. He never backed away from his sense, discovered as a young boy, that he didn't deserve to be mistreated. The violence of racism remains a factor in all of our lives: that *benign* color line kept my mother's two families apart, determined my school, destroyed the Crystals' house, sent Bob to Mississippi, structured my medical school, and today marks the abandoned territories of the inner city. The violence of the color line is what must be appreciated as we near the end of the century.

With what do we counter such an evil force? My dad was proud to be able to present his testimony to the veterans of the NNLC that, as promised, he had retreated to the ghetto and come back strong. But he saw the cutting edge of the destruction of the ghetto itself. He lived in fear of the economic genocide he saw coming. He understood that urban renewal had unleashed yet another kind of killing force. He was almost shrill at times in his efforts to share his vision of the apocalypse with those of us who would have to pick up the standard after he had departed. It was one thing to retreat to the ghetto and come back strong, but what if the ghetto itself was erased from the face of the earth?

None of what he saw, however, shook his faith in coalition. He believed that people must first find common cause with each other.

Beyond that beginning he knew that people could come to love and respect each other, based on common experience.

But this is not easy. On either side of the color line exists a mentality of abandonment. Both the abandoner and the abandonee are prone to adopt the attitude, "I don't need to care about you, I just need to take care of myself." The narcissism of partition is a particularly insidious and enduring injury to the collectivity of human beings. We will not overcome that nasty individualism quickly; meanwhile, we live with the dangerous consequences of disregard.

A Pittsburgh city councilman, at the close of World War II, proposed that a particularly inviting bit of real estate—the closest residential community to downtown—be "revitalized" and the current occupants displaced. In demolishing the area nothing of any social value would be lost, he averred. Nothing of his, that is. But the black people who lost their homes to his land grab still mourn the lively community they once had. How many families were set adrift like the Crystals and the Ollies? How many other families suffered, domino-like, from the displacement of their friends?

How is it possible to look at a community and see "nothing of social value"? I pose this as a psychiatric question, because the action of seeing "nothing" where there is "something" requires some form of mental acrobatics. Seeing place comes from habit and exists largely outside our consciousness. We learn to see buildings and roads and schools, but then we cease to notice them, too busy carrying out work to think about the structures that support our activity.

What, then, is the habit that looks at a community and sees "nothing of social value"? This redefinition of the question is useful, because we know how to outline the components of habit: action, reinforcement, repetition. We can easily imagine that as a boy that councilman had looked across the color line and been told, "Just no-count colored people. Not to worry yourself." And so the habit was initiated. Without occasions for the councilman to meet colored people and to learn that they mattered, the habit remained unchallenged until one day it became city policy.

The corollary of "only what I see matters" is "I can push you off your land." Thus the radical narcissism of one individual disrupts the attachment of another, planting in that second person the seeds of disdain. Like any contagion, disconnection spreads through the populace. How do we know this? We know this because people are buying bigger cars, building bigger houses, and creating more garbage just at a time when they should be living ever more lightly on the earth.

Bears, raccoons, and coyotes have begun to encroach on suburbs around the nation, causing consternation to the residents. "Get rid of the animals" has been the general reaction. But the animals were tenants of the land long before William Levitt dreamed up subdivisions. Why must they leave? Does the partition between people and nature not have the same evil effects as other lines and walls?

The psychology of place is essentially about belonging. Because it is a fundamental part of human psychological makeup, we know that all people need to belong. Each and every human being needs a place to call *home*. And because we are not that different from other living organisms, we can reason by extension that all living creatures need a place to call *home*. The radical narcissism that permits some people to take the homes of other people also allows them to claim the land without regard to the needs of other living beings. Just as my dad as a boy on the Eastern Shore of Maryland was enraged by the assault on his garden, so all people and all creatures are enraged by attacks on the integrity of their homeplace. In the short run it is possible to push people around and to run the bears and the raccoons off the land. But in the long haul that cannot be the way: it just won't work.

It's a lot easier to say, "Only what I see matters." Then you don't have to worry about recycling or child safety seats or abandoned houses or even other people. It will be hard to take the path of sharing. We will need support and nourishment of a new kind. Black Elk told us that "Everything the Power of the World does is done in a circle." The problem with a circle is that it could be another kind of line. Can we imagine, instead, a spiral that taps the power of the circle but incorporates the openness to change that is required if we are to learn to share?

Take tomatoes, for instance. If I simply grow tomatoes every summer, I follow in the cycle of my father and his father before him and his father before him. This is good, but it lacks the power to protect and transform the land. What if, instead, I join with all of my neighbors. Each of us has only a tiny plot of land, but among us we might have enough land to share fruits and vegetables all summer long. I would be happy to give away the surplus of tomatoes that I have in August in order to receive some zucchini in return. I don't know how to start such a spiral, but I can already hear, in my mind's ear, the strange stories we would have to tell ten years from now, after we have walked in each other's gardening shoes.

I am a dreamer, perhaps, but I see little choice between my spiral of hope and the coming apocalypse. Displacement will be the problem of the twenty-first century, more wrenching and more injurious to the human spirit than even the color line. But it is not a necessary future. Greed is a prominent feature in human nature, but we need not give in to it.

Years ago, Orange city councilman Ben Jones told his fellow councilmen that they had to vote for a new high school. He said then, "I submit that if we fail to pass this resolution, it will be more expensive than any of us ever dreamed." The time had come, he insisted, for them to say *yes*.

Those words linger for each of us. The right to a place is a sacred right, a right of each living being on the earth. If we fail to acknowledge that, the costs will be more than we can even dream.

The time has come.

Say *yes*.

NOTES

INTRODUCTION

1. Deborah Tall, *From Where We Stand: Recovering a Sense of Place* (New York: Knopf, 1993).

2. Bowlby's "personal and familiar environment" is what I am referring to as "near environment." Bowlby argues that "many of the difficulties that have dogged psychiatric and psychoanalytic theories of anxiety have arisen because insufficient recognition has been given to the enormous role that an individual's personal and familiar environment, including his familiar companions, plays in determining his emotional state. Only when it is realized that each man's environment is unique to himself can how he feels be understood" (John Bowlby, *Separating: Anxiety and Anger,* vol. 2 of *Attachment and Loss* [New York: Basic Books, 1973]: 148).

3. Leighton comments that "It has been noted that the objects for which people strive are enormous in number and diversity. . . . The multiplicity of objects is easily seen even in such fragments of lives as have been presented here. . . . Tom Young wanted security in his home, a roof over his head, and protection for his wife and children. He also wanted the love of his family and the good opinion of his neighbors. His farm was a means to these ends, but it was a means to another end too. It was a chance to create something — develop his stock, grow his produce, and bring order out of the tangle of nature" (Alexander H. Leighton, *My Name Is Legion: Foundations for a Theory of Man in Relation to Culture,* vol. 1 of *The Stirling County Study of Psychiatric Disorder and Sociocultural Environment* [New York: Basic Books, 1959]: 135–47, here 147).

4. See especially Kai T. Erikson, *Everything in Its Path: Destruction of Community in the Buffalo Creek Flood* (New York: Simon and Schuster, 1976); Anthony F. C. Wallace, "Mazeway Disintegration: Human Perception of Sociocultural Disintegration," *Human Organization* 16 (1957): 23–27; Edward

Relph, *Place and Placelessness* (London: Pion, 1976); Anssi Paasi, "Deconstructing Regions: Notes on the Scales of Spatial Life," *Environment and Planning A* 23 (1991): 239–56; Mary Bishop, "Street by Street, Block by Block: How Urban Renewal Uprooted Black Roanoke," *Roanoke Times and World News*, January 29, 1995, special section; and Christopher Alexander, *The Timeless Way of Building* (New York: Oxford University Press, 1979). I think it is fair to say that all of these authors approach issues of place with a strong interest in process. One of the most influential of those arguing such a position is the writer-activist Jane Jacobs, author of the classic *The Death and Life of Great American Cities* (New York: Random House, 1961).

5. Relph, *Place and Placelessness.*

6. Paasi, "Deconstructing Regions."

7. The great African-American scholar, W. E. B. Du Bois, wrote, "The problem of the twentieth century is the problem of the color-line,— the relation of the darker to the lighter races of men in Asia and Africa, in America and the islands of the sea" (W. E. B. DuBois, *The Souls of Black Folk* [New York: Signet Classic, 1995]: here 54).

1. IN RETREAT

1. Ernest Thompson and Mindy Thompson, *Homeboy Came to Orange: A Story of People's Power* (Newark: Bridgebuilder Press, 1976).

2. Mindy Thompson, *The National Negro Labor Council: A History*, Occasional papers of the American Institute for Marxist Studies, ed. Herbert Aptheker, no. 27 (New York: AIMS, 1978). This paper is a history of the National Negro Labor Council that I wrote as an honors thesis while at Bryn Mawr College. Dr. Aptheker, who was my thesis adviser, later published it.

3. Ernest Thompson, "Homeboy Talks to Train in Detroit," from a 1970 audiorecording of a reading by Dr. John Alexander. This reading took place as part of a reunion of former members of the National Negro Labor Council, held in Newark, New Jersey, December 12 and 13, 1970. Quotations in this section are transcribed from the audiotape, which is in the author's possession.

4. I met Arleen Ollie through Mary Bishop, a journalist with the *Roanoke Times* who has written extensively about the collapse of the inner city (Bishop, "Street by Street").

5. Communication from the Essex County Department of Education to the Orange Board of Education, 1964, quoted in Thompson and Thompson, *Homeboy*, 124–25.

6. Anthony Imperiale played a significant role for many years in leading white racists in the Essex County area. Late in life, he had a vision of the Virgin Mary, which precipitated a renunciation of his former views. Interestingly enough, he complained that he was having a hard time making a living. It appears that *anti*racism is not as lucrative as racism.

7. Alexander, O'Neil, White, and Glover quoted in Thompson and Thompson, *Homeboy*, 151.

8. John W. Alexander, "In Memoriam," quoted in Thompson and Thompson, *Homeboy*, iv–xiii, here iv, vi, xii.

2. LOVE-TORN

1. *Bulfinch's Mythology*, ed. Richard Martin (New York: HarperCollins, 1991): 47–53.

2. In this chapter and after, verb tense distinguishes the conversations that occurred in the real time of the stories from commentary on the past made during the writing of the book. Story conversations are in the past tense, commentary in the present tense. Occasionally the stories refused to stop in the past, which complicates the rule. At such points I beg the reader's indulgence.

3. U.S. House of Representatives Un-American Activities Committee, Hearings on Communism in Detroit, quoted in M. Thompson, *NNLC*, 32.

3. WAYLAID

1. Robert Coles, *Children of Crisis: A Study of Courage and Fear* (Boston: Little, Brown, 1967).

2. Steffens, who is eloquent on the change made in his life by having a horse, notes on this point, "I never played 'follow the leader,' never submitted to the ideals and the discipline of the campus or, for that matter, of the faculty. . . . I think I learned this when, as a boy on horseback, my interest was not in the campus; it was beyond it; and I was dependent upon, not the majority of boys, but myself and the small minority group that happened to have horses" (Lincoln Steffens, *The Autobiography of Lincoln Steffens* [New York: Harcourt, Brace, 1931]: 25).

4. ADRIFT

1. Charles Elliott, *The Transplanted Gardener* (New York: Lyons and Burford, 1995): 187. Elliott's own experience of transplantation certainly heightened his sensitivity to the problem.

2. Erikson, *Everything in Its Path.*

3. Erikson, *Everything in Its Path,* 187–88.

4. Erikson, *Everything in Its Path,* 196–97.

5. There is growing literature on the long-term effects of the Buffalo Creek disaster. Two useful articles are Bonnie L. Green, Mary C. Grace, Jacob D. Lindy, Goldine D. Gleser, Anthony C. Leonard, and Teresa L. Kramer, "Buffalo Creek Survivors in the Second Decade: Comparison with Unexposed and Nonlitigant Groups," *Journal of Applied Social Psychology* 29 (1990): 1033–50; and Paul Simpson-Housley and Anton de Man, "Flood Experience and Posttraumatic Anxiety in Appalachia," *Psychological Reports* 64 (1990): 896–98.

5. RESURRECTION

1. C. S. Lewis, *The Lion, the Witch and the Wardrobe,* vol. 1 of *The Chronicles of Narnia* (New York: Collier, 1970).

2. Nancy A. Anderson and Mary J. Roman, "The Double Image: Women and Minority Students at P&S," report to Dr. Bernard D. Challenor, associate dean, and Dr. Bernard Schoenberg, associate dean, October 1977. Photocopy of the original report in the author's possession.

3. Anderson and Roman, "The Double Image," 12.

4. Anderson and Roman, "The Double Image," 34.

5. Although I have ancestors from many "racial" groups, I have more than one drop of "black" blood, which by U.S. standards makes me "black." To the extent that the world operates by categories, I've been treated as a member of the black group. My interior view includes this reality of ascription, along with a host of other realities that reflect my mixed heritage and complex daily life.

6. "The Psychiatry of Racism and Poverty" Group, Final Report (College of Physicians and Surgeons, New York, 1976): 4. Holographic original in the author's possession.

6. IMMERSION

1. A photograph from this series by Steve Schapiro appears on the cover of the book by Doug McAdam, *Freedom Summer* (New York: Oxford University Press, 1988), and another has been used by the Ford Foundation in its promotional material for the full-length documentary film, *Freedom on My Mind: Voter Registration in the South*.

2. Alfred Lord Tennyson, *Idylls of the King* (London: Penguin, 1983): 214.

3. McAdam, *Freedom Summer*, 68.

4. McAdam, *Freedom Summer*, 70–71.

5. McAdam, *Freedom Summer*, 71.

6. Tennyson, *Idylls*, 206–7.

7. Fullilove Family Trip Diary, 1988.

8. Kathleen Norris, *The Cloister Walk* (New York: Riverhead Books, 1996): 4.

9. Alice Kaplan, *French Lessons: A Memoir* (Chicago: University of Chicago Press, 1993).

10. Kaplan, *French Lessons*, 142.

7. FOUNDLINGS

1. Gertrude Chandler Warner, *The Boxcar Children* (Niles IL: Albert Whitman and Co., 1972).

8. FIRST PLACE

1. Black Elk, as told through John G. Neihardt [Flaming Rainbow], *Black Elk Speaks: Being the Life Story of a Holy Man of the Oglala Sioux* (Lincoln: University of Nebraska Press, 1972): 194–95.

9. HOMESTEADING

1. Abe Chanin with Mildred Chanin, *This Land, These Voices* (Tucson: Midbar Press, 1977): 5.

2. Jonathan Kozol, *Rachel and Her Children: Homeless Families in America* (New York: Crown, 1988): 63. The quote from Angie is one segment of a discussion among a group of homeless children living in a squalid welfare hotel. The discourse Kozol recorded ranks high among truly powerful conversations, for it reveals the awful instability of the children's world, the dangers that surround them, and the fears that consume their lives. Angie's vision is frankly apocalyptic: "I think this world is ending. Yes.

Ending. Everybody in the city killin' on each other. Countries killin' on each other. Why can't people learn to stick together? It's no use to fightin'. Fightin' over nothin'. What they fightin' for? A flag! I don't know what we are fightin' for. President Reagan wants to put the rocket on the moon. What's he doin' messin' with the moon? If God wanted man and woman on the moon He would of put us there. They should send a camera to the moon and feed the people here on earth. Don't go messin' there with human beings. Use that money to build houses. Grow food! Buy seed! Weave cloth! Give it to the people of America!" (65).

3. Man-Ho Kwok with Joanne O'Brien, *The Feng Shui Kit* (Boston: Tuttle, 1995).